INSPIRED BY THE BEATLES

AN ART QUILT CHALLENGE

Donna Marcinkowski DeSoto

Schiffer Publishing Ltd

4880 Lower Valley Road • Atglen, PA 19310

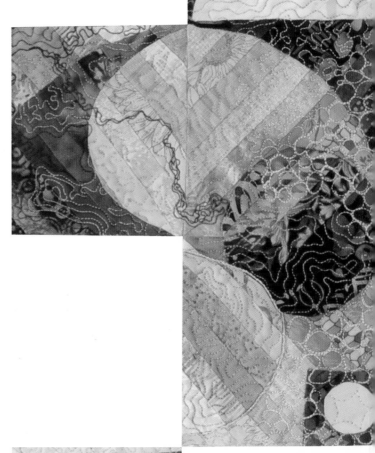

DISCLAIMER

This book is not sponsored, endorsed or otherwise affiliated with The Beatles, Apple Records, the Estate of Michael Jackson, Sony/ATV Music Publishing, EMI Music Publishing, or any of the companies whose products are mentioned herein. These products include Bose, LEGO, Lutradur, Timtex, and Tyvek, among others. This book is derived from the author's independent research.

DEDICATION

This book is dedicated to God, in thanks for a multitude of blessings He has given me and for the extraordinary people He has put in my life.

CONTENTS

FOREWORD

Remember when you first heard the Beatles? Were you dancing in a dorm room? Singing along with the car radio? Screaming at a concert? No matter where, you felt that pure joy of their music … Music that expresses our hopes and dreams, and gives us refuge and peace … Music that grabs the soul.

Like musicians, visual artists also experience the wonder of creating art. We express our hopes and dreams while finding solace and joy. We stitch our soul into our artwork. We even share the same lexicon of terms as musicians. We talk of rhythm, color, contrast, and harmony.

So what better way to celebrate the Beatles' music than with visual renditions of that music? Like John Lennon said, "Music is everyone's possession." By translating their glorious music into fiber art, we try to capture that moment when we first heard a Beatles song and knew it touched our soul.

We, as fiber artists, love our Beatles! We love their gift to us through their music — and we celebrate them in the best way we know how with our own colorful rhythms and harmony.

So tap your feet, sing along, and shout "yeah, yeah, yeah!" Mostly, though, just enjoy the show.

Laura Wasilowski
Elgin, Illinois

ACKNOWLEDGMENTS

This book exists because of the help of an army.

I am indebted to my family. My husband Kurt gives me the opportunity to do the things I love. After long, stressful days at work, he comes home with growing regularity to a bowl of cold cereal for dinner. He doesn't mind the dining room table, buried somewhere under mountains of cloth. He still calls me "Honey," looking across the stacks of fabric at my face, so often lit by the soft glow of a 15-watt sewing machine light bulb. He ignores the dust and he doesn't question my mysterious road trips to Purcellville. I apologize for these distractions, thank him for his infinite patience, and promise to find more interesting cereals at the grocery store. My daughter, Aimee, is quite simply my angel whose compassion paints my world. My son, Andy, is digging me an early grave, but he is a steady source of encouragement and pride. My Mom and Dad are always there; I am thankful for their constancy.

To everyone whose art fills the following pages: Thank you for showing up, for doing the work, for bringing along friends and family, for your time, imagination, and enthusiasm in taking a chance on a little art quilt challenge that grew and grew and became this major project.

To Jennifer Weilbach: Thank you for being my right hand, my first responder, and my Yoda.

To my sister, Sandy Veatch; Thank you for your companionship and your eagle eyes.

To the friendly and efficient staff at Schiffer Publishing, Ltd.: Your website welcomes first-time authors and this book is proof that you are sincere in that invitation. I am grateful.

To the growers of coffee beans: Thank you.

To my mentors: Thank you to Mary Kerr, who first urged me to pursue this endeavor with this publisher and provided time and assistance with photography and counsel throughout; and thank you to Cyndi Souder, who shared her time to give heartfelt advice and sound wisdom. She was also most generous with her students, as many of their quilts appear on these pages.

To the Commando Skirts: Norma, Paula, Marsha, and Mary Lois, your steadfast commitment and support has made me a better person.

To my Playgroup sisters: Thank you for making it every Monday morning to spend time. We are bound together by our love of quilting, but it really is about so much more than the quilting, isn't it?

Last, but not least, to Paul, Ringo, George, and John: Thank you so very much for the enduring gift of your music. The familiar refrains of your songs and lyrics continue to delight and inspire.

One of my most favorite memories of high school happened in my best friend's basement. Taffy Miller taught me to play the piano. It was just one song, but we spent hours together, playing an endless loop of "Heart and Soul." No matter what drama the day delivered, all was well, sitting at her old piano, playing the duet, over and over. I love music and I can't imagine even a day without it. From Grandpa Patsy, singing "O Sole Mio" in his wine cellar, to "We May Never Pass this Way Again" at high school graduation, to "Santa Wants A Tuba for Christmas" at the Millennium Stage of the Kennedy Center, there is something about a song; it can magically whisk me away from wherever I am and take me back in time. I am captivated by melodies and lyrics by an ever-growing number of artists. One of the constants throughout my life has been music by the Beatles — their songs are timeless, thought-provoking, and inspiring.

Inspiration. For some, it's looking far beyond the breaking waves at the final burst of rosy glow, just as the sun slips below the horizon at the end of the day. For others, it might be a poem, a story in the news, a photograph, a change of seasons, or a certain peace that settles while having coffee with a friend.

When baby Joyce was born, I was inspired to make her a soft sage and peach-colored floral quilt. My parents' 50th Anniversary led me to collect a vast array of vibrant fabric printed with rich swirls of gold metallic threads and make them a king-sized, intricately-pieced Blooming Nine Patch quilt. I grew up surrounded by cherished icons and statues of the Catholic church. Once, during lunch at a new restaurant with friends, I got the funny idea to make a quilt that became "Our Lady of the Salad Bar." I have also made somber, little fiber art pieces based on Hurricane Katrina and another depicting the flooding in Boulder, Colorado. My first "art quilt" was created several years ago when I woke up to the news that our country had just bombed Baghdad.

Whether driven by exuberant joy or by a sick feeling in the pit of my stomach, the need to put needle and thread to fabric is my way of coping…my way of finding sanity in a world that oftentimes just doesn't make sense. I share this passion with many.

Art comes from inspiration. One of the ways fiber artists find inspiration is by participating in a group challenge. Someone, somewhere, announces an idea and comes up with guidelines. In early 2013, I asked several members of the Playing Outside the Block quilt group ("Playgroup," for short) if anyone had an idea for a new challenge. The one person who took my call for suggestions to heart was Jennifer Weilbach. She e-mailed me a unique list of ideas discovered, in part, from a quick search on the Internet. I read them all and one jumped right off the page: "OK, Feb. 2014 is the 50th anniversary of the Beatles USA tour."

Details and rules of the challenge were quickly determined. Each participant would choose a song from a master list of Beatles' songs, with no duplicates allowed. Each finished quilt had to measure 24" x 24" and could not contain any copyrighted images or lyrics. The quilts were to have a hanging sleeve and label attached to the back. The due date was August 5, 2013. There was no cut-off date to join, as long as participants delivered their quilt by the deadline. I put together a list of Beatles' songs and an announcement of the challenge was made to the Playgroup. In just six months' time, the "Fiber Beatles Project" became this collection of one hundred and fifty quilts inspired by the Beatles.

Over the years, I have come to trust Playgroup to rally and produce. What no one realized was how this idea would "go viral" and spread from Fairfax, Virginia, to points north, south, east, and west. Friends encouraged friends, and all who wanted to participate were welcome. Along with the bounty of quilts born from this challenge came a special camaraderie; the Beatles Art Quilt Challenge linked us together while we busily planned and made our quilts. The Internet made it possible for those at a distance to make introductions, share ideas, and spread joy and enthusiasm.

The first Beatles songs claimed were some of the most popular tunes. An entire collection could have been gathered from quilts of just four songs: "Yellow Submarine," "Octopus's Garden," "Blackbird," and "The Long and Winding Road." The extensive list of three hundred songs provided something for everyone. Many participants re-discovered songs they had forgotten or discovered others they had never heard before.

The quilts featured in this book contain a wide variety of techniques, styles, and interpretations. The interests, background, and skills of the artists are as broad as the assortment of Beatles songs. Some participants worked quite literally with the song title while others closely examined the deeper meanings contained in the lyrics. Criteria for participation was not artistry or craftsmanship, although those can't be denied; instead, these are emotional responses of where the Beatles' music takes people.

However, this book isn't just about the quilts. In the following pages, you will get to know the artists through both common and varied personal narratives describing the influence of music on their lives as fiber artists. Something remarkable I discovered in writing this book was how many of the artists sat, transfixed, on February 9, 1964.

According to the website www.edsullivan.com, a record-setting seventy-three million people, over forty percent of every man, woman, and child living in America, tuned in to *The Ed Sullivan Show* that night — that was 45.3% of households with television sets in 23,240,000 American homes. Our recollections are told on these pages again and again, almost as a refrain.

Just as participants in this fiber arts quilt challenge, *Inspired by the Beatles*, used songs to provoke creativity, I hope readers will likewise find inspiration in the words and art contained in this book. Please enjoy our visual rendition of the era-defining music that is the Beatles.

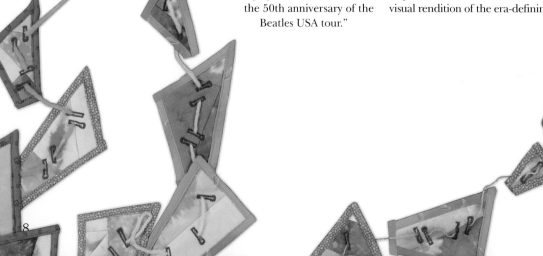

"A DAY IN THE LIFE"

Eileen Doughty • Vienna, Virginia

Eileen was only eight years old when the Beatles released their popular album *Sgt. Pepper's Lonely Hearts Club Band*. She distinctly remembers sitting on the floor of her living room, next to the stereo console, which was the size of a coffee table, looking at the album cover and listening to the songs over and over. She was fascinated by the lyrics and the stories they told. She also remembers hearing these songs on the radio, when they were brand new. This was when she started to become conscious of songs on the radio. Young, innocent, and oblivious to the problems in the world, this was also when she first started to develop her own likes and dislikes.

Eileen played the flute from elementary through high school and dabbled in the trumpet. Her best friends were in the school band. She played in the town band for a few years as an adult, and made her two kids play in band, orchestra, and take piano lessons. She believes reading music and playing an instrument should be required life lessons, just like learning to swim.

Eileen listens mostly to classical and classic rock music now. She is not afraid to admit that The Monkees and The Association are also on her iPod. "The 1970s was the best decade for music!" she says, adding that her favorite music to play to help her get in a creative mood is "Cinemix" — online radio that plays orchestral movie music. "It's calming and emotionally evocative."

Commercial cottons, lamé, organza, Tyvek™, ink, colored pencils; machine-pieced, appliquéd, and quilted, hand-appliquéd, fused, images manipulated in a photo editing program and printed on fabric, border design based on window architecture of Royal Albert Hall.

Eileen describes her mom as a wonderful seamstress who made most of her four daughters' clothes when they were young. However, Eileen didn't enjoy sewing, which she took as part of her home economics class in middle school, and didn't sew again until after college. Now, she wishes she had learned from her mom while she was still at home, she says.

In the 1980s, Eileen's mom took a quilting class and had so much fun that Eileen took one, too. They have been quilting ever since. Shortly after her first class, which was a traditional, completely hand-stitched sampler, Eileen began making art quilts. When she learned quilts didn't have to be geometric blocks, "it was an epiphany," she laughs.

Eileen chose "A Day in the Life" because of the imagery in the lyrics. The song is also on her favorite Beatles' album, *Sgt. Pepper's Lonely Hearts Club Band*. She says she quilts because it's so tactile and she's in continuous contact with her medium.

Eileen worked for ten years for the U.S. Geological Survey in cartography. She loves landscapes; that is her preferred theme in art-making. She is also ending her career as an at-home mother because her youngest child recently left for college. A member of the staff for Studio Art Quilt Associates (she's their website coordinator), Eileen is also president of the Potomac Fiber Arts Guild. Her artwork is in private, public, and corporate collections, and her work has been exhibited on five continents.

"A HARD DAY'S NIGHT"

Laura Brown • Austin, Texas

Cotton fabric, fusible interfacing; fabric printed, machine-pieced and quilted.

Laura considers herself a Beatles fan, even though she didn't grow up in the era of the Beatles. She has a cat whose name, Kitty Ramone, can be traced back to the surname Paul McCartney used when checking into hotels to mask his real identity.

Trained in classical piano while growing up, Laura played the flute in a youth orchestra. She mostly listens to indie rock now. Music puts her in a great mood and she especially loves singing to her young daughter. After Ivy was born, Laura started taking guitar lessons. Ivy had colic as an infant and singing to her was one of the ways she was able to calm her when nothing else worked, Laura says.

Laura's mom has been sewing all of her life. Laura took her first sewing class when she was thirteen years old. She was introduced to quilting at the age of twenty, when her grandmother asked family members to each make a block for a baby quilt for a new cousin. It was only one block that Laura made, but she was hooked. When she moved to Austin after college, she took her first quilting class at a local quilt store and has been quilting ever since. She began making art quilts as soon as she found out there were such things.

Laura has always loved art; she has drawn and painted her whole life. After moving to Texas, she attended the International Quilt Festival in the fall of 2000, where she saw for the first time quilts could

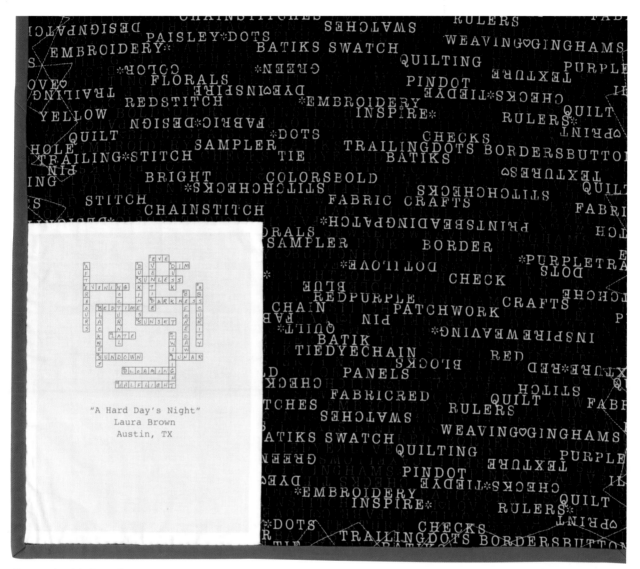

"A Hard Day's Night"
Laura Brown
Austin, TX

Reverse of quilt by Laura Brown.

be works of art. Walking among the quilts in that show, Laura confides, she felt like she was in an art gallery. Now, she quilts because it's like a form of meditation. It requires such focus that she is able to forget the rest of the world around her for a while.

Laura selected "A Hard Day's Night" because she thought it would be a challenge to come up with something to depict a hard day. It was indeed quite a challenge. She says that thinking of what to do actually took much more time than the actual making of the quilt did. "But it was part of the fun," she insists. Laura decided to make a Sunday crossword puzzle, since Sundays are typically the "hard day" for daily crosswords. All of the answers for the puzzle she

made are synonyms for the word "night." She utilized her typical style, which is simplistic and clean, and sang this song in her head the entire time she made the quilt. A special thing happened during construction of "A Hard Day's Night": Laura worked on her quilt while visiting her mom in Virginia, which gave her mom lots of precious bonding time with Ivy.

Laura is a two-time cancer survivor. She was diagnosed with ovarian cancer at the age of eighteen and has struggled with recurrent skin cancer. She loves national parks — her dream is to one day visit all of them, she says, adding that she's already been to a third of them. She also loves movies and confesses to being a chai addict.

"A SHOT OF RHYTHM AND BLUES"

Meggan Czapiga • Bethesda, Maryland

Cotton and batik fabric, plastic vinyl, ultra-suede, lamé, Swarovski crystals, nail heads, embroidery thread, stickers, ribbon; raw edge appliquéd and machine-quilted.

Though Meggan listens to the Beatles and loves some of their songs, she doesn't consider herself a diehard Beatles fan. When she and her sister were children — she was eight and her sister was twelve — they loved the *Sgt. Pepper's Lonely Hearts Club Band* album. They listened to it over and over in their unfinished upstairs bathroom because they could turn up the volume and dance on the plywood floor. Meggan adds that it was "lots of fun looking at that album cover" because it was so interesting.

Meggan took ballet and tap while growing up and had a choreographed dance number to "Octopus's Garden" for a spring recital. Her mother helped her sew the costumes and Meggan was so proud. For months, she dressed up in her treasured costume and danced to the song in front of her parents in the living room. She even wore the costume for Halloween that year.

When she was younger, Meggan participated in swing choir and played the clarinet. She is now involved in Middle Eastern dance. She listens to classical, oldies, hillbilly rock and roll, and alternative music. She has music playing most of the time because "it always picks me up and motivates me to finish difficult tasks."

Meggan has been quilting for a little over ten years. While she was growing up, her mother quilted and her sister did beading, cross-stitch, and other crafts. Meggan wanted to have a photo memory quilt for her bed, so she decided to make one for herself — and she has been quilting ever since.

She started making art quilts about eight years ago, Meggan says, when she felt the urge to combine her neuroscience background with quilting. She loves quilting and science so much that it seemed only natural to combine the two in some way. Her first art quilt was dedicated to the human brain. It is a two-sided quilt containing a neural network on one side. She quilts because she doesn't get a chance to be creative at her day job, Meggan explains. She uses her left brain at work and needed to find something to occupy her right brain.

Meggan took part in this project because she wanted to be involved in a challenge based on song titles, and she immediately knew what this quilt would look like when she read the title. As a research scientist who has been working in the immunology field for twelve years, "A Shot of Rhythm and Blues" was the perfect inspiration to incorporate a scientific theme into an art quilt, she says, and this piece is typical of her work because it is very detailed and has lots of sparkle.

Meggan listened to "A Shot of Rhythm and Blues" a lot while she planned and made her quilt. She always challenges herself when she makes an art quilt, and in this one, the challenge was in the details. She wanted the instruments to look as realistic as possible, she says, confiding that it took her twelve-and-a-half hours to make the music notes. She put a lot of time into this quilt — and loves the result.

Meggan can't imagine her life without sewing. She worked on this piece on the weekends and laughs that by the end her house was very dusty. However, she ignored the housework, as well as her other usual weekend errands, and her family ate out a lot. There was no food in the house because she didn't even go grocery shopping.

Besides working and quilting, Meggan does beading, makes pincushions, and enjoys experimenting with photo transfer techniques and fabric. She and her husband love to take pictures. Her awards and publications are all science-related. She volunteers for Operation Kid Comfort, which donates photo-transfer quilts to children of deployed servicemen and women, and makes quilts for babies in the NICUs of several hospitals all over the United States.

Meggan also volunteers in the Elephant Herpesvirus Lab at the Smithsonian's National Zoo in Washington, D.C. Working in collaboration with John Hopkins University, this lab is the prime worldwide resource of herpesvirus information, testing, and research for the global elephant community.

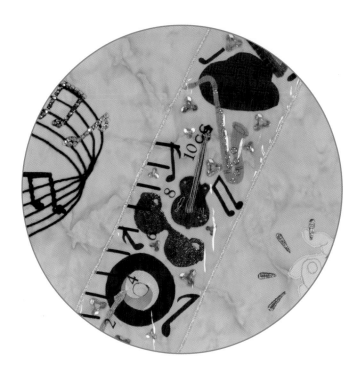

Susan R. Palfey • Fairfax, Virginia

Cotton fabric, various threads; reverse raw edge and fusible machine-appliquéd, machine-pieced, and quilted. Special thanks to Janet Palfey for her assistance.

Susan became a Beatles fan when she received a middle school history assignment to listen to music from pre-1975. Her parents were happy to oblige her by sharing their albums, tapes, and CDs. Prior to that, Susan had listened to Top 40 music at the gym where she was a gymnast. Her favorite Beatle is Ringo and she collects Beatles memorabilia.

Susan played the viola and took art through the end of middle school, but eventually decided to drop viola because she needed to take a foreign language in high school as her elective. As part of her college experience, she is taking art classes and is considering changing her major to scientific illustration. She has an Etsy site where she sells t-shirts and watercolor and acrylic paintings of animals.

Susan chose the song "A Taste of Honey" because it appears on the album *Please Please Me*. "The album that made me a Beatles fan," she notes. The song's warm tones and mention of honey inspired the quilt's color scheme, as the honeycomb stitching in the background communicates a theme of honey. The subject is a couple about to kiss — a taste of honey refers to the sweetness of a kiss. Susan chose plain fabric for the background and patterned fabric for the couple to define the subject matter and emphasize the simplicity of the song. This is her first quilt design, and Susan confesses that the profile of the young man highly resembles her boyfriend.

"ACROSS THE UNIVERSE"

Margie Werntz • Annandale, Virginia

Cotton fabric, metallic thread; Louisa L. Smith's Strips 'n Curves strip-pieced technique. Machine-quilted by Su Gardner.

"The truth is, I am far too old to be an avid Beatles fan," claims Margie. By the time the Beatles appeared on the American scene, she says she was fully immersed in Dr. Spock, Mother Goose, and other lullabies. Her granddaughter, Jane, was born in 1996, and Margie became her full-time nanny. She bought a Beatles cassette for the car to keep Jane amused on errands and, together, they learned to appreciate the Beatles.

Margie chose the song "Across the Universe" for this quilt challenge to commemorate a special event. In 1957, on the third date with her future husband, Carl, a physics grad student and amateur astronomer at the University of Minnesota, he offered to show her the moon. What could be more romantic? she thought. Carl lugged a five-foot, homemade telescope from his boarding house to a parking lot adjacent to the university field house and set it up. Within five minutes, they were captured by spotlights and surrounded by campus police, who thought they had a bomb. ("Would you believe they had bomb scares back then?") In the end, the police shared a closer look at the moon. That same telescope has traveled on many moves and each time it served as the perfect icebreaker to get to know their new neighbors. Margie and Carl have been married for fifty-five years.

The universe theme appealed to her because it gave her a chance to practice a new technique, Margie confides. She had recently finished her first large quilt using the "strips and curves" piecing technique, so, to create the strata for the universe piece, she used many half-inch strips of fabric. Special templates were used to cut the design elements from the strata. Margie left her comfort zone in doing this method of carefully matching all of the tiny strata seams with curved seams and by also matching strip seams from one 4" block to the next, all the while, projecting the "feel" of the universe.

"ACT NATURALLY"

Patricia Scott • Edmonton, Alberta Canada

Cotton fabric; fusible appliquéd, machine-pieced and quilted.

Patricia chose to make her Beatles quilt based on the song "Act Naturally" because she still remembers listening to it when she was young. Before beginning the quilt, she played the song again and paid close attention to the lyrics. They inspired the theme of a filmstrip.

Patricia is currently a project manager at an architecture firm who enjoys playing the piano. She listens to most kinds of music and says music brings her a lot of energy. It also stimulates her inspiration, or a feeling, which sometimes enables her to see a different perspective, she explains.

Patricia has been sewing since high school, when she discovered the fun of making her own clothes. She started making art quilts just over ten years ago. Art quilting, she relates, challenges her to express herself and to make her ideas come to life in fabric. If she didn't sew, she would have another creative outlet: watercolor painting, cross-stitching, or knitting.

"AIN'T SHE SWEET"

Dian B. Epp • Spotsylvania, Virginia

Cotton fabric, tulle, vintage rickrack; collage-quilted technique as inspired by Susan Carlson.

Dian listens to classic rock, oldies, and classical music because it is relaxing and brings great enjoyment to her life. Listening to music while she sews allows her to be free and spontaneous. She learned to sew from her mother when she was young. Dian sewed clothes, including her wedding gown, her children's clothes, and sport jackets for her husband. She has been making art quilts for nine years.

Dian chose the song "Ain't She Sweet" because one of her fondest memories is of her father singing the song to her and her sisters when they were children. In planning this quilt, she confides, she thought about her own sweet granddaughter. The photo she has on her desk of her granddaughter wearing over-sized sunglasses reminded her of many photos she had seen of the Beatles in sunglasses. Dian wanted to try to quilt a portrait and used this song, and the photo of her granddaughter, for inspiration. She challenged herself to use a monochromatic color scheme; she chose pink since it is her granddaughter's favorite color. This seemed to be a great way to stylize the quilt similar to the Beatles' album cover, *Let It Be*, where color-enhanced photos were used. As she worked on this quilt, her vision didn't go as originally planned, she explains, because the quilt had some ideas of its own.

A social worker in private practice, Dian can't imagine a life without sewing. If she didn't sew, she says, she would "shrivel up and fade away."

"ALL I'VE GOT TO DO"
Anne Winchell • Oak Hill, Virginia

Commercial and hand-dyed cotton fabric; photo transferred, machine-quilted.

When Anne saw the song title, "All I've Got to Do," on the Beatles art quilt challenge playlist, she instantly came up with a vision for a quilt. Her life as both a quilter and an accountant helped to form the idea of depicting two sides to her fictional desk, with a computer on one side and a sewing machine on the other.

Anne has two businesses. In addition to doing taxes, she has an online fabric store. She has sewn a little throughout her whole life, Anne explains, but she got really hooked when she and her mother began watching *Simply Quilts* on television.

"ALL MY LOVING"

Dolores McGlynn • Fairfax, Virginia

Cotton fabric; hand-appliquéd.

When he was in Vietnam in 1968, Dolores's late husband wrote home everyday. She still has the book of his letters to show for it. She chose "All My Loving" because he included this song on a tape he sent to her from Vietnam; it has been a favorite ever since.

Dolores listens to Celtic, gospel, country, and folk music, which, she says, can be soothing or exciting, depending on where she needs to be. She listens to music when she sews because it can be thought-provoking when she *has* to think, "which is not too often anymore!"

It is a mystery to Dolores as to why she quilts. She took a class through the county twenty-five years ago and has been quilting ever since, she explains. When she isn't quilting, she reads about quilts, shops for fabric to add to her stash, and talks to friends about quilting. She says that if she didn't sew, she would probably drink.

"ALL TOGETHER NOW"

Laura Wasilowski • Elgin, Illinois

Hand-dyed cotton fabrics and embroidery threads, batik fabric; fusible appliquéd, hand-embroidered, machine-quilted.

Laura's love of the Beatles' music stretches back many decades. There is always a tune in her head. Her earliest memories are of her sister being miffed with her for constantly singing, resulting in her mom telling her sister to "leave her alone!" Once she was in college, Laura's roommate woke her up every morning with "Here Comes the Sun" played on her record player. This was the only way to get her out of bed for an 8 a.m. class. Now, she listens to anything from country to blues to classical guitar. As an author, professional quilt maker, and quilt teacher, she writes and sings parodies of songs when she presents lectures on quilt-making.

Most of Laura's art is whimsical, stylized, and pictorial in nature, so when designing "All Together Now" she began by visualizing people joining hands. Soon, those people were running in a big circle and having a great time as they danced to this song. Laura confides that her favorite part was dressing the dancers and decorating their clothing with embroidery stitches. The quilt became a game from childhood because it was like playing with paper dolls, she says.

Laura learned to sew as a child in a Colorado 4-H Club. The 4-H ladies taught her how to construct garments, which led to a work/study program at the costume shop in college. She hand-dyed and printed fabric for garments when a neighbor introduced her to the world of quilt-making in the late 1980s. Laura realized that she could take the fabrics she was making for garments and use them to make art quilts. Today, she makes art quilts not only to earn money to support her family, but also to satisfy a creative urge to express herself in fabric, Laura explains. She enjoys entering her work in exhibits, and she is an award-winning artist whose work has been featured in many books and magazines.

Laura says she is happy when she creates artwork and often bursts into song while making a piece. She constantly hummed "All Together Now" as she made this quilt.

"ALL YOU NEED IS LOVE"

Maria Wilkins • Bumpass, Virginia

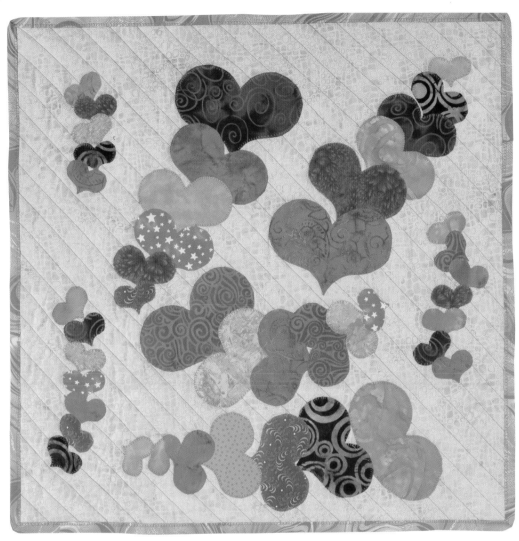

Cotton fabric; machine-appliquéd and quilted.

At one time, Maria had all of the Beatles records. She remembers sitting in front of the television with her family, watching *The Ed Sullivan Show*. When the Beatles performed for the first time, the thing Maria most noticed were the hairdos. The kids in her family thought the Beatles were cool, but her father just sat with his mouth open in complete shock.

Maria and her sister joined the foreign service and were sent to Bogota, Colombia, for two years when they were in their mid-twenties. They found a great first apartment there and immediately threw a party. The Beatles' music was going strong, perhaps too strong, because right after that they were evicted. Next, they rented a house where they continued the parties, and the Beatles' albums played and played. "Beatles' music never gets old," she says.

Eventually, Maria married and her husband bought her a Bose® stereo system, which she now has in her sewing room, so she can play music that won't ruin his tweeters or woofers. He never complains when she plays her Beatles' CDs.

Maria took oil painting classes for twenty-one years and then tried watercolors, which, she recalls, was a huge mistake. She became depressed and didn't want to paint anymore, but she needed something creative to do. When Maria retired from her job as a technical editor for a group of engineers, she started taking quilting lessons.

She chose "All You Need is Love" because it is one of her husband's favorite songs. Maria is proud to say that unlike other quilters who may have many incomplete projects, when she begins a project she finishes it before she starts another. She enjoys working with a time limit and having deadlines. When she's not quilting, she enjoys gardening, cooking, traveling, and all kinds of jokes, as long as they don't involve politics or religion.

Cotton fabric; machine-embroidered and hand-quilted. Embroidery designs from Apex, Bernina, Cindes Embroidery Design, Designs by Sick, Embroidables, Embroidery Library and S. Embroidery, with permission.

When everyone else was crazy about the Beatles, Cheryl wasn't because, she confides, she isn't a "joiner." She ended up enjoying their music later in her life than when it first appeared on the music scene.

Cheryl says music brings happiness and fun to her life, as well as inspires the recollection of fond memories. She sang in the chorus and played the E-flat alto horn and trumpet in high school. Today, she loves listening to classic country and oldies from the '50s and '60s.

Cheryl first started sewing in high school because she wanted to make her own clothes. She began creating art quilts two or three years ago, Cheryl explains, after seeing them in magazines. She especially loves making children's quilts. Not only does she make them for family and friends, but one of her favorite projects is to make quilts for the Armed Services YMCA Kid Comfort Program. These quilts are for children of deployed armed services members if the parent makes a request. She also donates quilts to cancer patients and blankets for animal shelters. Cheryl believes the addition of embroidery designs to these quilts makes them more special and using an embroidery machine gives her many extra options while stitching.

Cheryl's career was in business analysis. In addition to quilting, she is interested in crocheting, oil and acrylic painting, gardening, and reading.

"AND YOUR BIRD CAN SING"

Sandra Starley • Moab, Utah

Cotton fabric, rickrack, shoelace, buttons; machine-pieced, appliquéd, and quilted.

Sandra is a Beatles fan, but doesn't consider herself hard core. She is more of a Paul McCartney and Wings fan who also enjoys rock, pop, indie, and country music. Music elevates her mood. Although she is more likely to listen to the television when she sews, she loves the music in her Zumba classes. She fondly remembers seeing the *Yellow Submarine* movie as a little kid while visiting her grandparents. She wishes she could have heard the Beatles play live, especially after seeing a Beatles tribute band once in concert.

In designing this quilt, Sandra says she wanted to capture the feel of the song, which is light-hearted and silly. The design became whimsical and folky, as did the colors and materials, all of which were inspired by the music and lyrics.

Sandra is a criminal defense attorney and a quilting professional. She appraises quilts, collects antique quilts and quilt history, writes a regular column on quilt history for the National Quilting Association's magazine, *The Quilting Quarterly*, teaches classes, designs patterns, and does antique quilt trunk shows nationally. Almost every quilt she's made has been for a challenge.

While she was working on this quilt, Sandra was in a car accident and broke her hand, which had a significant impact on her life and on this quilt. Ironically, the song describes the bird as "broken." She came to see the bird on this quilt as once broken, but now healed. Sandra wasn't able to do much sewing with a splinted hand, but her sister Donna came to the rescue and machine-appliquéd for her. Sandra confides that the experience helped her to let go of her usual need for control and accept help in order to get the quilt done.

"ANY TIME AT ALL"

Mary Lois Davis • Bee Cave, Texas

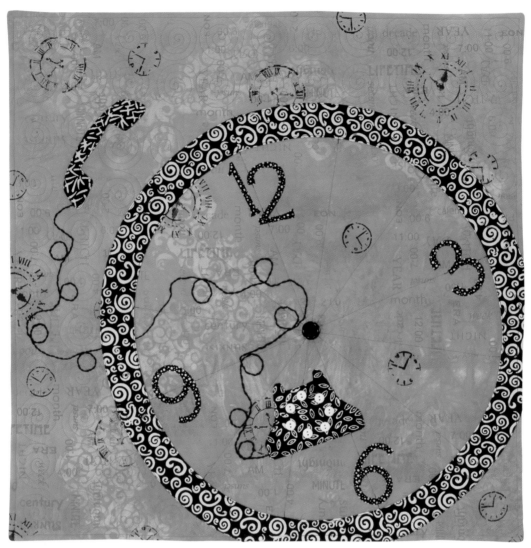

Hand-dyed cotton, batik, silk thread, buttons, paint; hand-dyed background fabric, discharged color, thermofax screen printed, raw edge appliquéd, couched, free motion quilted.

Mary Lois has been a big Beatles fan for many years. She first saw the group on *The Ed Sullivan Show* on a teeny-tiny black and white television screen and has been bobbing her head along to their music ever since. She also listens to '50s, '60s, and '70s, classical and liturgical music. While she is making art, she prefers to work in silence, but otherwise music brings her joy and peace, as well as the occasional toe-tapping and hand-jiving.

Mary Lois doesn't remember the first time she picked up a needle and took a stitch, but she learned purposeful sewing at age nine when she joined 4-H and made an apron. While attending Colorado State University, she studied economics with an emphasis on textiles and clothing; some of her educational background has been very helpful in all of her stitching. Her creative process and skills grew tremendously when she studied creative embroidery in the City and Guilds program while living in England for four years.

The song "Any Time At All" resonated with her. Throughout thirty-five years of marriage, her husband has traveled extensively for his career. He was in Singapore when their daughter had her one and only automobile accident. He was in England when they had a three-foot snowfall in northern New Jersey. He was in France when monster bees invaded their house. He was on his way to Italy when the terrorist attacks on 9/11 occurred. The list goes on. Despite it all, he has always been at the other end of the telephone. Mary Lois has called him all over the world at every time of day and night and struggled with several languages in order to leave a message for him to call home. She doesn't remember there ever being a day during his travels when he did not call home. All she had to do was call — *any time at all* — and he was there.

"BABY'S IN BLACK"

Allison F. Whittier • Ellisville, Missouri

Cotton and flannel; photo transferred, machine-pieced. Machine-quilted by Pam Cole.

Allison loves music by the Beatles. She recalls sitting with her sister and their mom back in the mid-sixties. They were brushing her mom's short dark hair over her face so she would look like one of the Beatles.

Music has always been an important aspect of Allison's life. When she was a little girl, she collected music boxes. Every night she would wind a box or two over and over again until she finally fell asleep. Later, when she was in school, her father told her she would do so much better if she could just learn her studies as well as she memorized the lyrics to the songs she listened to. "Life would be dull without music," she says.

When Allison was young, she played the viola in the school orchestra. Her brother played the cello and her sister played the violin. The three of them put on mini-concerts for their parents until her brother switched to the saxophone. They finally had to stop because every time he played the sax, their dog started barking.

In 2007, Cece, a good friend and seasoned quilter, asked Allison if she wanted to join a few friends in taking a quilting class. The first thing Allison made was a chair rail quilt for her father. Since then, this group has met every Thursday. Allison says she's always amazed to see the finished quilting project, even if it's quite simple, and still considers herself a novice quilter.

"Baby's in Black" features her children — Michael, Christopher, and Lauren. The idea of this challenge appealed to her because she knew it would push her to do something for herself, which is something she doesn't do often, Allison explains. She has been very focused on her children lately, "so it was nice to have something to take me away from all of the craziness." She put a Beatles' playlist on her iPhone to listen to while she worked on the quilt, and says joining in the fun of this challenge has been a wonderful experience.

"BACK IN THE U.S.S.R."

Priscilla Stultz • Fairfax, Virginia

Assorted fabric, crayons, markers, pens; sketched, colored, and machine-quilted.

Priscilla's suite mate in college played "Why Don't We Do It In the Road" nine thousand times a day. Even though she still doesn't like that song, Priscilla is a Beatles fan. The first song her future husband ever played for her was "Strawberry Fields Forever."

While she was making this quilt, Priscilla sang "Back in the U.S.S.R.," but luckily no one else was home. "I can clear the church when I sing," she laughs. This is something her kids tease her about. She travels whenever she has the opportunity, but she hasn't gone to Russia yet. It is on her bucket list.

"This quilt was a joy to create," Priscilla says. "Once I began work on it, everything came together beautifully, from the sketch to the quilting. The quilt almost made itself."

Priscilla began sewing at the age of seven, doing hand-stitching that her grandmother taught her. Another great influence was 4-H. She won a ribbon in the county fair when she was ten for a wool needle case she made shaped like a dog. Once she had kids, she made quilts for their beds, but never used a pattern. Her interest in art quilting began when she made a colláged vest that started out as a quilt. It won an "Honorable Mention" award at the Mid-Atlantic Quilt Festival. Since then, her garment creations have walked the catwalk several times over the years. Before she turned fifty, she had made 500 charity quilts. She is an award-winning seamstress who continues to take classes to learn new techniques and find inspiration.

For Priscilla, quilting is like breathing; it defines her. If she didn't quilt, she says, she would work on improving her golf swing, which is terrible.

Cottons and cotton blends, upholstery fabric, foam, various fibers, fabric paint; machine-appliquéd, painted, machine- and hand-quilted, embellished.

Audrey can remember singing a few Beatles songs back in the day, but her older sister was more of a fan. Now Audrey listens to rhythm and blues because of the calming effect it has on her life. At times, the music is also thought-provoking. She usually doesn't listen to music when she is creating, but it does generate creative ideas in the planning stage.

Audrey chose the song "Bad Boy" because it isn't a love song, as most Beatles' songs are. What attracted her to this art challenge is that it sounded unique; she also wanted to test her skills. Her son, Jamel, is a graphic artist, and he helped design and create this quilt.

Together, she explains, they found it challenging to figure out what the quilt needed to tie it all together, but they also enjoyed finding the solution and the way to accomplish what they wanted to convey. Even though he co-produced this quilt, Jamel is not really interested in quilting. However, he does offer feedback and assistance on many of her other projects, Audrey says.

While completing this quilt, Audrey put aside art quilt class homework and unfinished quilts. She enjoys singing, traveling, and socializing. And if she didn't sew? "I would paint, do pottery, and travel more instead."

Sandi Goldman • Annandale, Virginia

Commercial and hand-painted cotton fabric, silk organza, various threads; photo transferred, machine-pieced and quilted.

Sandi is a Beatles fan who grew up in the sixties. Her earliest Beatles memory is seeing them on *The Ed Sullivan Show* and being so excited about their music, the hysteria surrounding the Fab Four, and how cute they were. Nowadays, she loves to listen to a variety of music in the car, but when she's at home working on her art, she tends to enjoy the peace and quiet of her thoughts.

As a child, Sandi watched her grandmothers knit, crochet, and cross-stitch tablecloths. She remembers teaching herself to embroider the pockets of her jeans. She also learned to knit as a child. She believes all of this influenced her to major in textile design at East Carolina University.

Sandi's career in art began at a yarn store in Old Town Alexandria, where she taught weaving. She is still an avid knitter. Next came a stint in the graphics world, then motherhood, and now she is firmly entrenched in the fiber art world. She shares a studio at the Workhouse Arts Center in Lorton, Virginia, with ten other fiber artists, where she

is able to create in a beautiful space, show her work, and teach. She says when she read the words to "Because" they fit perfectly with the six photos from a trip to Alaska that had been on her design wall for a year. This style of quilt is typical of her work; it evolved from a class she took from artist Donna Radner. The class introduced Sandi to art quilting and completely changed the way she makes quilts.

Sandi is active in a program at a local hospital that teaches women on bed rest with high-risk pregnancies to quilt and knit. She makes quilting kits for them with donated supplies and has been passionate about this project since it began three years ago. She also teaches quilting at a local cancer center where clients immerse themselves in creating pieces with the calming effects of fabric.

Sandi is involved with the Quilt Alliance, which preserves the stories of quilters and their quilts, is a committee member of Sacred Threads, and belongs to Fiber Artists @ Loose Ends, a small group dedicated to making quilts for healing spaces.

"BEING FOR THE BENEFIT OF MR. KITE"

Karen Wolfson • Chantilly, Virginia

Cotton fabric, ultra-suede, beads, wool, ribbon; paper pieced, hand and fusible appliquéd, embroidered.

Karen first heard the Beatles' music at a physics summer camp. One of her roommates was obsessed and played their records constantly. Later, Karen had to buy *Rubber Soul* and *Revolver* just to cope with the withdrawal after camp ended. Karen still listens to the Beatles; she says they have never been in such eclectic company, since she also listens to alternative music, video game soundtracks, and anime soundtracks.

Karen has no musical ability of her own; in fact, she is famed for her lack of musicality. In middle school (where band was a mandatory elective), she was assigned the triangle. There was never a part for the triangle in anything they played, so her job was to stand there and not play. Likewise, she is only allowed to sing if she is alone in a car on a deserted highway and even then she has to "drive faster than 45-mph to outrun

the shame." Every now and then, though, she just has to belt out a tune.

Karen chose the "Mr. Kite" song because of three words in the lyrics: calliope, sound, and collage. Her quilt features penguins throughout because she likes penguins. In fact, she says she's surprised everyone else isn't constantly making penguin-themed quilts. She is grateful to all of those quilters in her guild for donating their leftover scraps of fabric because she used those scraps to make this quilt.

A high school physics teacher, Karen explains that she quilts to help her calm down and for the joy of applying math to the real world. She also enjoys that it allows her to have a moment to herself, though she ended up having little of that when her husband decided to get in on the action (see "Maxwell's Silver Hammer" quilt, page 110).

"BÉSAME MUCHO"

Susan Fernandez • Fairfax Station, Virginia

Susan says she is a Beatles fan because they wrote the best lyrics. She listens to most types of music, especially rock and roll from the '50s to present-day, classical, blues, jazz, country, and alternative. As a customer advocate manager in information technology, Susan spends a lot of time in the car commuting to and from work. She doesn't know what she would do without music to help the time go by. Music takes her to a better place, soothes and calms her, and sometimes energizes her to do more, she says.

When she and her husband, who is in the military, got married, one of the highlights of her first trip to meet "the family" in Puerto Rico was a gathering where his great-uncles, all professional musicians, performed. It was at Christmas and the entire family was there. This was one of the last times the great-uncles performed as a group.

"Besamé Mucho" had long been a family favorite, and her husband's grandparents, aunts, uncles, and cousins eagerly awaited her reaction and approval when they sang this lovely ballad. To their delight, she loved it because of the soulful lyrics and melody. "Bésame Mucho" became a favorite. In selecting this song, Susan was glad for the opportunity to transform a daily endearment and a beloved song into a work of art. "Bésame Mucho," or "Kiss Me A Lot," evolved into larger-than-life art lips with a little "flower power and psychedelic" influence.

Hand-dyed and painted vintage linens, lace, merino wool roving, silk shibori, batiks, Angelina, beads; hand-dyed and cold reactive dyed, painted, wood block printed, free motion embroidered and quilted, beaded.

To hear Susan tell it, she was born with a needle in her hand. She first learned to sew as a young girl with lessons from her mother, grandmothers, and aunts. She made doll clothes, knitted, crocheted, tatted, and even attempted to make hairpin lace. Her sister still has a knitted cat she made for her, complete with shoes, bonnet, and eyelet pinafore. The cat is a little scary-looking, but her sister loves it because it was made especially for her. Susan studied clothing, textiles, and related arts in college, which is where she made her first two quilts. She designed and made wedding and christening gowns for family and friends, and also sewed upholstered cushions for butcher-block style furniture that she made with her husband when they were first married.

Susan has been making art quilts since she joined Art Quilt Journey classes four years ago. Her art quilt education has included applying techniques learned from other great quilt artists: Judy Gula's hand-dyeing techniques, Lyric Kinard's screen and discharge printing, Liz Kettle's

stitching and embellishment, and Jamie Malden's block printing. Though still a novice, Susan says her voice continues to evolve with each new quilt.

Besides stitching, she enjoys gardening, cooking, interior design, and photography, as well as visiting new places and experiencing life's gifts with her husband, family, and friends.

Cotton fabric, silk dupioni, rickrack, pompom trims, grosgrain ribbons, birthday blow-outs and scrapbook decals; photo transferred, machine pieced and raw edge fusible appliquéd.

Yes, yes, yes…Marjie is a Beatles fan! Because she grew up in the "boonies of Casper, Wyoming," she never had an opportunity to see a Beatles concert ("Rats!"). However, she still remembers how excited she was when they appeared on *The Ed Sullivan Show* when she was just ten years old. She had the biggest crush on Paul.

Marjie still listens to the Beatles, as well as New Age (Mannheim Steamroller, Enya, Yanni), jazz (Kenny G, Nat King Cole, Natalie Cole), music from the Big Band era, '50s music, Frank Sinatra, Simon and Garfunkle, Three Dog Night, the Nitty Gritty Dirt Band, and Herb Alpert and the Tijuana Brass, to name just a few. Music revs her up, especially when she cranks up the volume on a favorite song like "Joy to the World."

Marjie chose "Birthday" because it was the first song she could picture in her mind. She discovered during the process of making this challenge piece she likes making memory quilts with old photos. The baby pictures of her two sons, Charlie and James, and the adorable picture of James in a Halloween clown costume inspired this quilt. She wants everyone to know she was up until 5 a.m. on the day of the deadline finishing it.

Marjie's mom taught her how to sew when Marjie was in the sixth grade. Her favorite things to make were stuffed toys for her room, including a huge patchwork turtle for the floor. Today, Marjie says, she quilts because she loves the bright, wonderful fabrics that are available.

Marjie's work career began as a statistician for the Federal Highway Administration. Eventually, she helped her group as a research fellow at LMI to develop applications for NASA and the aviation community.

"BLACKBIRD"

Su Gardner • Fairfax, Virginia

Cotton fabric; raw edge appliquéd, hand pieced and machine quilted.

Reverse of quilt by Su Gardner.

Su is a Beatles fan, but doesn't have any Beatles stories to tell because "I'm too young." She played the piano and sang in a choir when she was a child. She prefers to listen to disco and soft rock now and says music keeps her cheerful and motivated. When she's trying to be creative, though, music is actually a distraction.

About twelve years ago, Su was looking for a new hobby and so she started sewing. She began by making Hawaiian shirts for her husband and home décor accessories. She made her first art quilt six months ago and finds quilting to be "relaxing and fun," but says she hasn't developed a "style" yet. She has been a professional longarm quilter for the past three years and the machine quilting she does for her business keeps her very busy, she explains. Art quilting has allowed her to meet more quilters than she ever thought existed.

When Su told her husband about this challenge, he chose "Blackbird." She wasn't familiar with the song and needed to research the lyrics and their meaning — she listened to the song over and over again for inspiration.

Two hobbies Su had before she took up quilting were making doll house furniture and small-scale train layouts. If she wasn't sewing, she reveals, she'd do those things again and would also spend more time working with her bonsai and orchid collections.

"BLUE JAY WAY"

Frieda Anderson • Elgin, Illinois

Hand-dyed cotton fabric by artist, silk and rayon thread; fused collage, machine-quilted.

Frieda loves the Beatles, and although John was her favorite while she was growing up, she says these days "I'm a real fan of George." She listens mostly to classic rock, folk, contemporary, classical, blues, and '50s and '60s music that includes Frank Sinatra and Tony Bennett.

Although she has no musical background, other than singing in the church choir when she was in parochial school, Frieda listens to music everyday. When she works in her studio, music helps her to relax or to get pumped up and be creative, she explains.

Frieda loves to make things. She has been sewing since she was eight or nine years old. She started as a traditional quilter, but very quickly moved over to the "dark side" and became an art quilter because she wanted to create her own designs. She adds that she quilts because she loves color and fabric. She has been making a living as a working artist and teacher for more than fifteen years.

Frieda reveals that she chose the song "Blue Jay Way" because of the lyrics. She envisioned "going up the hills in Hollywood on a foggy day" to find a friend's house. Her typical style is represented here, as she makes a lot of landscape quilts through fused collage, working with her own hand-dyed fabric. She adds that she especially likes the design of the fields and plans to use this layout again. Before making the quilt, though, she had to dye the color gradations that she needed for her background. She explains that she wanted something "soft and foggy-looking." Since she usually works in very bold colors, this was a bit of a departure for her.

Frieda has won several national awards for her quilts. Not only is she the author of three books on dyeing fabric and fusible quilt collage, but her work has appeared in multiple magazines and books. She has also given television interviews about her quilts and has made several instructional DVDs.

"CAN'T BUY ME LOVE"

Dana Brennan Hancock • Chantilly, Virginia

Cotton fabric, rickrack, beads, plastic coins; machine pieced, appliquéd and quilted, beaded, couched.

The first LP Dana owned was a Beatles record. In junior high and high school, she played the flute, oboe, and bassoon. She had a very short solo for one important concert; she was to play the first bars of "Hey Jude." Imagine a quiet auditorium and then an oboe playing those first few bars, which would have sounded wonderful, says Dana. Unfortunately, she couldn't play loud enough and a saxophone player had to assist her. She recently enjoyed Paul McCartney's concert in Washington, D.C.

Before this challenge, Dana already had several pieces of fabric in her stash depicting money and immediately had design ideas for "Can't Buy Me Love." The upper corner of her design depicts piano keys, a guitar fret, and drumsticks on a drum. She confesses that she

hadn't done much machine-appliqué or beading on quilts before this, so she enjoyed experimenting and including these new techniques.

Dana's mother taught her how to sew clothes in junior high school. She remembers sewing and listening to music, including Beatles songs, especially during the summer. Of course, she sang along. Dana says she enjoys the creativity of quilting, as well as the beautiful fabrics. She also finds other peoples' quilts to be very inspirational.

Among other things, Dana has worked as a teacher of English as a second language, at a brokerage firm, a city newspaper, and an accounting firm, and she has volunteered for various charities and schools. Besides sewing, she takes care of her grandchildren, knits, makes lace, beads, reads, and walks.

Nancy is most definitely a Beatles fan. She owned every album and 45 that came out; her favorite song is "I Want to Hold Your Hand." She remembers watching their first appearance on *The Ed Sullivan Show* with her thirteen siblings and her parents when she was a little girl. As a teen, she also remembers the huge controversy about the Beatles saying they were larger than God. "Yeow, why did John marry Yoko?" she recalls thinking. She also remembers the awful feeling she got when John was killed outside his apartment in New York City as she wondered, "Who would do such a thing?"

Nancy loves all kinds of music, but her favorite types are rock and roll, as well as music from the '60s, '70s, and '80s. Music has made a huge impact on her life. When she was young, she listened to the *Italian Hour* radio show on Sunday mornings while her mom made homemade spaghetti noodles, sauce, meatballs, chicken, salad, and apple pies. In her twenties, on Friday nights, she hung out at bars to dance the night away with siblings or friends; they also cranked up the tunes while washing her 1968 Bel Aire. Songs played at church, funerals, and weddings; music was everywhere. Today, she plays music in the background during dinners with family and friends. She teaches family and consumer science in high school and finds ways to incorporate music into her classroom. Music helps her students calm down and gets them into the "groove of how they will spend their next ninety minutes of class together."

Batik, cotton and lamé fabric, embroidery floss, stabilizer, lapel pin, printer fabric, pen; fusible appliquéd, hand sewn and machine quilted.

Nancy has been sewing for as long as she can remember. She used to lean on her mom's back and look over her shoulder while she sewed. The sewing machine was set up in their dining room. When she was old enough, Nancy's mom said she would buy her as much fabric as she wanted to sew her own clothes. Twenty-two years ago, when she moved from Ohio to Virginia, she wanted to make new friends and meet other mothers. She didn't know how to quilt when she moved to Virginia, but since she loved to sew, she thought this would be a great hobby to do with friends. Quilting "calms me down and stretches my creative thought processes," she discovered. She especially loves seeing her completed quilts being used by others. Later, her friend, Paula Golden, introduced her to art quilting in a Fractured Lone Star foundation class. She says she never considered herself an "artist" until she began to "break away from the traditional thought process of quilting" and started "pushing the boundaries."

Nancy reveals she almost didn't participate in this challenge because "so many of the 'good' songs were already taken." She found one called "Carol," looked it up, and listened to it on YouTube™. She didn't think it was a very catchy song, but she liked the storyline. Plus, she has a daughter named Carol. Carol's fiancé, Brent, suggested making the man shown on the quilt sitting at a bar, and Carol thought to show the back of her brown curly hair pulled up by a hair clip. Nancy envisioned Carol with her eye on Brent, but "there's another guy in the picture who just might steal her heart away. Brent sits at the bar trying to figure out how to get and keep this pretty girl, so he learns to dance and sweeps Carol off her feet." Thus, the boy gets the girl. (The back of the quilt has a silhouette of the couple dancing.) In completing this quilt, Nancy gives special thanks to Lisa Purdy, Kris Bishop, and Barb Scharf for their moral support and helping to sew on the binding.

When she isn't stitching, Nancy enjoys spending time with her husband, Jimmy, her three daughters, and young grandson, as well as golfing, playing Mexican Choo-Choo dominoes, gardening, gathering and preparing food, and traveling.

"CARRY THAT WEIGHT"

Beth Richardson • Alexandria, Virginia

Cotton, synthetic, and silk fabric, buttons; pieced, appliquéd, and machine-quilted.

When the Beatles first appeared on *The Ed Sullivan Show*, Beth's fifteen-year-old cousin insisted that the family watch the performance on their grandparents' TV because it was "the only color set we had." She doesn't remember what anyone else thought, but Beth loved the Beatles. She feels lucky to have seen them perform at the D.C. Stadium in 1966.

Beth says music has always been a part of her life. She listens to rock and roll, as well as some jazz and classical. It brings her joy and has helped her to get through some hard times, she explains. She found heartbreak songs especially meaningful when she had a broken heart. She has no musical background, and was a failed guitar student in junior high school because she didn't practice.

Participating in this challenge took her out of her comfort zone, Beth confesses. She chose "Carry That Weight" because the music to that song got stuck in her head. This song is the middle part of a medley that begins with "Golden Slumbers" and ends with "The End."

Beth was inspired to use gold on the bottom of the quilt because "Carry That Weight" grows out of "Golden Slumbers." The black mountain and dark colors symbolize the heaviness of the weight, "whatever it might be," she says. The lighter colors near the top show the movement toward the lighter feeling of "The End." Once she figured out what to do, the design flowed organically, taking twists and turns as she worked on the quilt. She hopes it "captures the feeling that many of us deal with as we go through life."

Beth has been sewing since she was twelve years old, when she made an apron in her seventh grade home economics class, and she's been making art quilts for about ten years. She started with a class on making fabric postcards. She enjoys creating with fabric, sometimes with beads and other embellishments added. Recently retired from her job as a Federal attorney, Beth also likes knitting, reading, baseball, and crossword puzzles.

"CAYENNE"

Stacie Northrup • Falls Church, Virginia

Cotton fabric; machine-appliquéd and quilted.

When Stacie was young, her family sang along with the Beatles on the radio constantly. She is a Beatles fan who likes "all kinds of music because it feeds my soul." She took piano lessons at an early age and later played the flute, piccolo, and recorder.

A specific melody accompanies her creative process for each project. This art challenge captured her imagination because she could picture the quilt to this instrumental song in her mind's eye. She likes to try different quilting styles to satisfy her curiosity, she explains, though she admits to experiencing frustration with her choice of techniques for this piece. Later, however, she was quite satisfied with how well the quilt ended up embodying her creative vision.

When she was young, Stacie made clothing for her dolls. She started making art quilts ten years ago because she "couldn't find any commercial quilting patterns that satisfied my ideas." Besides quilting, Stacie enjoys drawing, oil painting, knitting, crocheting, traveling, reading, and hiking. Everything else, however, was put on hold while she made this quilt. Now she looks forward to cleaning her house, reorganizing her sewing room, and finishing other projects.

Nancy B. Adams • Annandale, Virginia

Nancy is a Beatles fan who listens to a variety of music, though when she plans her quilts, she usually designs in a quiet room. Nancy thinks of "Chains" not as chains of oppression, but rather as representative of "two lives interlocked as love joins them more tightly together in time."

Nancy does all types of sewing and quilting. She likes traditional blocks that can be made into "sturdy, usable bedcoverings and original, needle-turned-hand-appliqué for wall art." This quilt is rather typical of her style because the appliqué and quilting are her usual tedious techniques to give the effect she desires. The chains, though, are unusual since she crocheted them from a variety of metallic cords and threads.

Nancy learned to sew at the age of seven; she earned extra cash by designing and selling doll clothes as a teenager. Her frugal parents taught her "homemade is better than purchased," so she has always tried to design her own projects. Needing bedcoverings and wall decorations was a good excuse to start a fabric stash as a newlywed.

Nancy taught herself to quilt in the 1970s as a lonely army bride, far from home. She says she enjoys the process of selecting fabrics and planning her designs. She makes quilts for others for pleasure and has made a bed-sized quilt for each resident at Sojourn House (a community-based, therapeutic group home for girls who are experiencing significant difficulties). She also donates lots of quilts to various organizations, such as the Quilts of Valor program. However, her most rewarding experience has been as a volunteer quilt teacher to hundreds of students, aged seven to seventy, over the years.

Nancy's work has traveled to national quilt shows, been published in magazines, and one piece was even purchased by the city of Columbus, Georgia, to send to their sister city in Japan. She enjoys sharing her ideas; it gives her a sense of pride knowing that others like her work, and she can't imagine a life without sewing and fabric. She quilts to "express myself," as well as to create beautiful, comforting, and useful items. "It's also a great social outlet," she adds. When she's not quilting, she loves traveling, hiking, watching birds, gardening, reading, cooking, and entertaining.

Velveteen, cotton, and other miscellaneous fabrics, metallic cords, and threads; crocheted, machine-pieced and quilted.

"CHRISTMASTIME IS HERE AGAIN"

Cathron Birge • Springfield, Virginia

Cotton fabric, buttons, yarn, ribbon; machine-pieced, appliquéd, and quilted, hand-quilted and embellished.

Cathron listens to the Beatles' music, but says she doesn't really consider herself a fan. She chose this song because her family loves Christmas and it's a fun time of year. What would Christmas be without a tree and Santa?

After Cathron had finished making her Beatles quilt, her older son came by the house. She showed it to him and said it might be traveling to be exhibited, possibly for as long as a couple of years. He mentioned somebody would really like to have it as a Christmas quilt. They dropped the subject and went out to dinner, where she told him that his sister and niece would someday inherit her grandmother's engagement ring. "He said, 'I think that's only fair. They get the ring and I get the Christmas quilt! I have no use for the ring, but I can really use that quilt!'" she recalls.

Cathron says the quilt was a tremendous amount of fun to make, and although she stopped everything to complete it, she is really glad she participated in this challenge.

Cathron started quilting when she was sixteen. Her best friend's mother taught her to use an old sewing machine. Before that, she had done needlework when she was six years old in school in Paris. She still has the embroidered bag she made with her name on it. She loves anything having to do with fabric because "it makes me feel relaxed," unless everything goes wrong. Now that her eyesight is slowly going downhill, she isn't able to do the intricate work she used to be able to do, she confesses. Still, she has to keep her hands busy. If she didn't sew, she says, she "would slowly go mad!"

"COME TOGETHER"

Kathy Lincoln • Burke, Virginia

Batik, beads; fusible appliquéd, machine-pieced and quilted, hand-beaded.

Kathy is a Beatles fan who sang in church choirs for many years. She listens to just about any kind of music except for rap. Classical to classic rock are her favorites. She appreciates music because it "calms me when I need some peace"; on the other hand, it can also "energize me when I need a little pep."

The inspiration for this quilt came from thinking about the Beatles, the chorus of "Come Together," and the time frame of the song. She participated in this challenge because it sounded like fun.

Kathy has been sewing since she was nine years old and quilting since a friend got her started in 1984. She says quilting gives her a creative outlet; she is also "happier when I'm playing with fabric," she confesses. She was once a medical technologist, but is now a quilt teacher and lecturer. Her quilts have been published in magazines and displayed in national exhibits. When she isn't quilting or teaching, she loves to read and garden.

Commercial cotton, hand-painted rickrack, various threads; machine threadwork, decorative bobbin work.

Linda wasn't a huge Beatles fan at first, but she loved the song "Sgt. Pepper" when it came out. She enjoys listening to classical, pop, and children's music. Her grandma taught her to play the piano when she was six years old. Linda started out as a trained biologist. Years later, she was a parent helper in her children's co-op preschool. One rainy day, she removed the "do not play" sign from a piano the school wanted to get rid of. She started playing nursery rhymes with the kids when the director suggested Linda apply for the music teacher job. She got the job, and her life changed. She still works as a preschool music teacher.

Linda says she participated in this art challenge because "I can't resist a challenge." When she saw the song title "Cry Baby Cry," she explains, "a lot of images came to my mind." She has a friend who does red work embroidery; she also had recently taken a bobbin work quilting class, which is how she decided to do her quilt.

When she was a young girl, Linda learned to sew from her aunt. She had a special doll and made clothes for her. She has been making art quilts for about twenty years. Judy House, and later Cyndi Souder and other wonderful teachers, have had a big influence on the quilts she makes. She quilts for "the sheer pleasure of it." She also enjoys watercolor, music, bridge, and Words with Friends. If she didn't sew, Linda divulges, she would go crazy and "maybe have a cleaner house."

"CRYING, WAITING, HOPING"

Nancy L. Evans • Jeffersonton, Virginia

*Cotton, lamé, tulle, polyester, beads, buttons, lace, beaded trim, ribbon, rickrack,
a feather, permanent ink, cotton and polyester threads; fusible appliquéd with
inking, hand-embellished, machine-quilted.*

Nancy has enjoyed singing along with the Beatles ever since their popularity came about when she was seventeen years old. She saw their performance on *The Ed Sullivan Show* and says the music drew her in and made her happy. Now, she also listens to popular, classical, bluegrass, jazz, country, and Celtic music, or to the sounds of the water, sea, and birds. Music has always fed her soul. She confesses "I can listen to any type of music and feel the emotions" of joy, sadness, calm, frenzy, funkiness, and seriousness and enjoy their diversity. She has loved to sing along to songs from the time she was very young and sang with her dad as he played the guitar.

Nancy generally quilts without music, as she prefers it to be quiet so she is able to listen to her innermost thoughts and can concentrate on her projects. However, while making this quilt, she exclaims, she listened to the Beatles music and had a great time singing along.

Nancy looked at the list of available songs and immediately had an idea of how she would interpret this particular song as a quilt. She had never heard "Crying, Waiting, Hoping" and listened to it on the Internet. There are few lyrics to the song itself, so she used the three-word title to inspire the child "crying," "waiting" in line for the ladies room, and the bride with her wedding ring quilt in hand "hoping" to be married

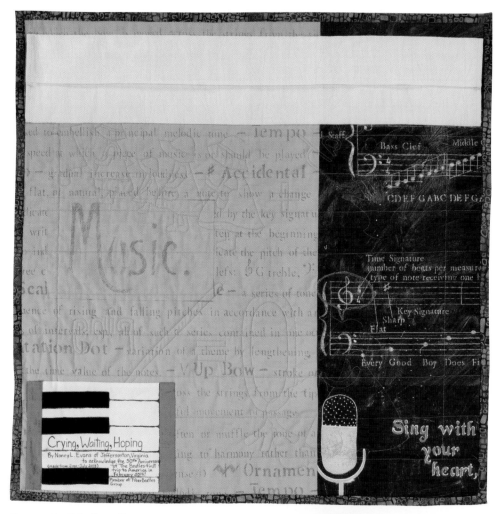

Reverse of quilt by Nancy Evans.

someday. While she was still working on the quilt, she received a surprise from her husband — he had ordered a special two-CD disc set entitled *The Beatles Live at the BBC*, which contained her song on disc one. A bit of trivia she learned is that the Beatles worked tirelessly for one day, July 16, 1963, recording eighteen songs for the BBC.

Nancy "jumped at the chance" to make a quilt to honor a Beatles song and had a lot of fun making it. She confesses she felt "humility and excitement" when she committed to this challenge, with faith going forward. She experienced an array of emotions during the process: disappointment when her first background didn't measure up, renewed faith with a new plan of attack, and then happiness when the last stitch was made and she could be proud of her effort. While she worked on her quilt, the housework and laundry waited until there were no clean clothes and she couldn't stand the dirty kitchen floor any longer. She even put off her youngest granddaughter Julie's week at grandma's house so she could finish the quilt first and not have time taken away from her.

Nancy began doing embroidery and crochet at around ten years of age with her grandmother. They made hand-sewn doll clothes together. In junior high, she took home economics, where she sewed a complete outfit using her mother's sewing machine. As for her beginnings in art quilting, a good friend wanted a landscape quilt for his dental office, so she and his wife designed a triptych of three seasonal landscape panels that now decorate a wall of his reception room. She quilts, Nancy explains, because it's a wonderful hobby that satisfies her need to give

part of herself to others. She also feels that it allows the "creativity I have been given by God" to be shown in fabric form.

Nancy is an award-winning artist who is an active member of numerous quilting organizations. She loves making quilts for soldiers and area shelters, and she makes surgery caps for children. Throughout her quilting career, she has taught students many techniques. She is proud that her eldest granddaughter, Abigail, has a stash of her own fabrics and has made two quilts that have been exhibited. She hopes Abigail will continue to quilt and pass this on to her own children and grandchildren.

"DAY TRIPPER"

Starla Phelps • Alexandria, Virginia

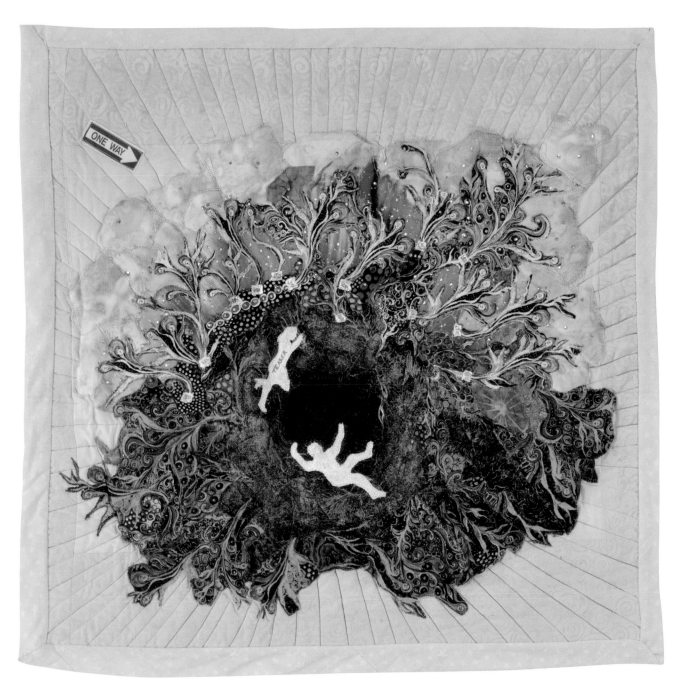

Cotton fabric, Swarovski crystals, paint; trapunto, painted, fused, machine-quilted.

Starla majored in several disciplines before obtaining her bachelor's degree. Her husband wanted her to take music appreciation for exposure to opera and classical music, but the professor decided to focus on the Beatles, Creedence Clearwater Revival, and other popular rock and roll artists. Her husband just shook his head. She loves most kinds of music, especially music from her past, the '60s and '70s, as well as country, bluegrass, jazz, Broadway, '40s and '50s, classical, and even some opera. Music brings back life memories and makes her want to dance and sing, neither of which she is good at doing. Music also sets the mood for her creative process and helps her to relax.

Starla's mother made most of the family's clothes. In junior high, Starla took home economics and made a skirt. Later, when she tried

Partial reverse of quilt by Starla Phelps

to sew at home, her mother said if she didn't follow her rules (press every seam, use a thimble), she wasn't allowed to use her machine, so she quit sewing. When she married and moved to Virginia, she didn't have any winter clothing. In desperation, she was forced to teach herself to sew. She went to Sears and purchased a basic sewing machine for $49. Next, she moved to California, where she attended design school. Upon her return to Virginia, she designed and made ultra-suede, wool, and silk clothing for businesswomen.

When Starla chose her song for this art challenge, there were not many left. "Day Tripper" would not have been her first choice, she confesses, but it really challenged her and now she's glad she got it. She went on a trip to Edinburgh and visited a strange shop where she saw the most unusual belt buckles. She bought several she thought might work on this quilt, representing the woman and drugs in the song. She had many ideas and several people made suggestions. At a local quilt show, she learned from three quilters she met who were knowledgeable about LSD that it came in three forms: pills, postage stamps, and sugar cubes. She marvels that it's amazing what you can learn at a quilt show! From that information, she found the perfect fabric and just let her mind

play. The quilt turned out to be nothing like she had envisioned. While she made it, she listened to "Day Tripper" over and over again. She likes to play and have fun when she is quilting, and this is reflected in her quilt.

Starla considers all of her quilts to be art quilts because she doesn't follow the rules and she doesn't use patterns. Instead, she just begins and hopes her visions work. She began quilting four years ago and her first quilt took over 2,000 hours to complete. An appraiser was unable to put a value on that particular quilt because she had never seen anything like it. Her next quilt, which was shown at the annual Porsche Convention Art Show, won "Best Fiber," "Best in Show," "People's Choice," and a "Crystal Bowl Award" from the Porsche family.

A Porsche race car driver for twenty-eight years, Starla is an instructor who loves speed and teaching drivers skills that can be used on the track and on the street. She hopes she has saved lives through doing so. In her former life, she worked as a CPA, but says she felt stifled as an accountant because real creativity in that job could "land a person in jail!"

Starla quilts because she loves fabric and color, and it gives her the opportunity to express her creative spirit.

"DEAR PRUDENCE"

Heather Foster • Petersburg, West Virginia

Cotton fabric, silk and cotton thread; hand and fusible raw edge appliquéd, hand- and machine-quilted. Special thanks to Nadine Duke, Heather's mother, for her help.

Heather became a huge fan of the Beatles in 2001, her junior year of high school. She listened to their music nonstop and read every book about the Beatles she could get her hands on.

Music has always been a major part of Heather's life. She began playing the piano at age five and went on to major in music in college. She also loves to sing. She still uses these skills, both recreationally and professionally. She has played in various pit orchestras, sung in several opera choruses, and performed in local theater productions.

Heather settled on "Dear Prudence" because she loves the song. A lovely and inspiring design took shape in her head as she was taken with some of the imagery in the lyrics. This is her first quilt. Her mother and mother-in-law both quilt, and she had resisted their efforts to make her become a quilter. Her mother knew her weakness, though, and told her about this Beatles art quilt challenge. As Heather sketched out the design, she realized the face in the sky is actually Prudence's spirit, meditating in the clouds and looking down on the scene below. The quilt turned out much more poetic and fitting than she had originally intended!

Heather learned many new skills while making this quilt, and says she is so grateful to her mother and mother-in-law, Darlene, for giving her access to their libraries, fabric stashes, and quilting knowledge. Her prior skills in drawing portraits gave her the confidence to tackle a portrait quilt. The face was done by hand: needle-turn appliqué using a fabric layering technique she learned from the book *Faces and Places* by Charlotte Warr Anderson.

Even though she still doesn't plan to make a habit of quilting, Heather admits she is on her way to becoming "one of those ladies who collect vintage machines." Her next project involves refurbishing her "new" 1947 Singer sewing machine. She also has a knee-controlled 1926 Singer, but she didn't use it for this project, she says, "because there is no way to sew slowly with it."

"DEVIL IN HER HEART"

Marilyn League • Memphis, Tennessee

Cotton fabric; paper-pieced, machine-quilted, hand-embellished.

Marilyn was just a young girl when the Beatles appeared on the music scene. She and her older sister were completely caught up in Beatlemania. The group seemed so exotic to two girls who lived in the hometown of Elvis Presley. The first time she and her sister saw the Beatles on *The Ed Sullivan Show* they nearly fainted. Her father, a jazz and big band musician, was less than impressed. He walked around the house for days saying, "yeah, yeah, yeah," in a slightly derogatory tone.

Today, Marilyn is a diehard rock and roll fan. She loves all of the music from the '80s and '90s. She jokes that iTunes® is like crack because whenever she has any extra money, she downloads music. If she is feeling down in the dumps, she turns on the music loud and dances like a teenager, which is guaranteed to lift her spirits. When the music is going and her machine is humming, she could sew all day

and night, Marilyn says. Her mind goes to a place where all things are beautiful and possible.

Whenever she participates in an art quilt challenge, Marilyn likes to give herself a personal creative challenge as well. This time, she made herself do paper piecing, a technique she now loves. She would like her friends Vanessa McCallum and Patricia Smith to know how much she appreciates their help, advice, and "faith in my abilities."

Marilyn claims she quilts because she has to — she can't imagine a life without sewing. A dressmaker by profession, she also enjoys mixed media, collage, art journaling, gardening, and, when she's hungry, cooking. Her work has been published in *Quilting Arts Magazine* and she is very active in both the Memphis Sewing Guild and the Memphis Association of Craft Artists.

"DIZZY MISS LIZZY"

Nysha O. Nelson • Bartlett, Tennessee

Cotton fabric, fabric paint; whole cloth, painted, trapunto, machine free motion quilted.

Nysha confirms he is a Beatles "admirer." He sang in a church choir growing up and had endless piano lessons that yielded little more result than draining his parents' financial resources. Music augments his mood: if he is happy, the right songs can boost that happiness into elation, while a sour mood can be improved by smooth music and thoughtful lyrics. He listens to pop, light rock, soul, rhythm and blues, jazz standards, and classical.

Nysha chose the song "Dizzy Miss Lizzy" because he is fascinated by mandalas, spirals, and all things circular. He listened to the Beatles' music as he designed this quilt, which features contrasts of high color and a spiraling nature. Nysha painted first, and then quilted with an aesthetic plan. When it was done, he stepped back and saw the final design. He realized that not only had he captured the spinning and dizziness he wanted, but the high/low texture and contrast were all present and it looked like his work married with the era of the song.

Everyone took home economics in the seventh grade and Nysha loved it. He continued sewing through high school and did costuming in college. He studied painting, but found his attention wandering. He turned his focus to sewing and quilting — that was seven years ago and he is in love! His career is now art creation and art education. He quilts because he loves the effect of light and shadow as it falls across the quilted surface; he finds this both invigorating and enticing. He also loves that every human has some relationship to fabric or cloth and, therefore, to the very heart of this medium.

Nysha's work has been included in a couple of books and he is the Kentucky/Tennessee representative for Studio Art Quilt Associates. He is a certified ZenTangle® instructor and looks forward to teaching in his new studio, beginning another whole cloth quilt, and resuming figure drawing with his sewing machine.

"DO YOU WANT TO KNOW A SECRET?"

Bunnie Jordan • Vienna, Virginia

Tea-dyed crinoline, cotton, embroidery floss; reverse and fused appliqué, machine-quilted.

Bunnie remembers having her girlfriends over to the house when she was young to watch the Beatles on *The Ed Sullivan Show* in black and white. She contends music can bring back memories; it can also soothe and relax or energize, depending on the need. Today, she listens to all kinds of music, everything from country to classical, with a lot of Motown, rock, and smooth jazz in between.

Bunnie acknowledges that she participated in this challenge because it sounded like fun. When she saw the title to this song, she immediately heard the song in her head. It was an early Beatles song and the first top ten song to feature George as a lead singer. Bunnie always liked George best. She opted for a pretty literal interpretation of the title so people could guess the song, using a photo of her son and daughter-in-law to depict the couple sharing the secret. She chose to do it all in black and white because when she first saw the Beatles perform it was in black and white.

Bunnie began sewing when she was in high school, but didn't start making quilts until adulthood, when friends needed some baby quilts. Art quilting seemed to evolve from traditional quilt-making for her, she explains, but she didn't consider it "art" back then. Today, quilting is an essential part of her life. She loves making quilts and seeing those made by others.

Bunnie is a registered nurse who also loves travel, reading, and yoga. If she wasn't making quilts, she'd probably take more art classes and do more quilt documenting and studying of antique quilts. She is a member of numerous quilting organizations. Her quilts and articles have appeared in magazines, and she has appraised quilts for more than twenty years. Bunnie co-authored the books *Quilts of Virginia* and *Quilters Hall of Fame*.

While everyone else was busy working on their Beatles art quilts, Bunnie was on vacation and spent a few days in Prague. There, she discovered the John Lennon Wall. Since the 1980s, protesters and graffiti artists have covered it with Beatles' song lyrics and images. Musicians still play Beatles music there and the graffiti continues in the spirit of peace and free speech. Bunnie notes that visiting this wall was a serendipitous way to do research for this project.

Photos courtesy of Bunnie Jordan.

Cotton fabric; fused raw edge and hand appliquéd, machine-pieced and quilted, photo transferred.

Kathy was aware of the Beatles when they appeared on the music scene, but they weren't considered cool in her little hometown of DeQueen, Arkansas.

Kathy enjoys the nature of a challenge. She says this one sounded like fun, adding, "Parts of it were." Kathy explains she doesn't do art quilts; she makes pictorial traditional quilts that tell a story. When she saw the song title "Drive My Car," she immediately imagined the design for this quilt. This song called to her on a personal level. Her grandbaby, Michael, is shown on the quilt, and he was eighteen months old when this photo was taken by his dad. Since Michael constantly tries to drive the family cars, Kathy's quilt direction was obvious. It would depict the ideal summer evening, with Michael getting one more turn around the yard before he has to come in. He, as all children should be, is the star in his family's lives, so the evening star shines down on him. (Kathy gives special thanks to her son-in-law, Jason Lamey, who took the photo of Michael Lamey, who is "driving" the car in her quilt.)

Kathy's sister, Mary, learned to sew in 4-H. She was a natural-born teacher and taught Kathy nearly everything she knows. Kathy is a mother who has been a teacher and an Army wife. Now, she is a grandmother and a professional longarm quilter. Quilting soothes her soul and makes her happy. Before she became a professional quilter, she won a few awards, but got too busy for the competitive circuit. As a professional, she teaches quilting while managing a fabric store. She has written a bi-monthly column for a quilting magazine, designed patterns for several fabric companies, and made models for those companies that appeared at Quilt Market and in print. Several customers have won numerous awards and their quilts, which Kathy quilted, have appeared in many books and magazines.

In her non-quilting life, Kathy is a committee chair with her chapter of the Daughters of the American Revolution and she works closely with active duty military and the USO.

"EIGHT DAYS A WEEK"

Diane Tansey Cairns • Springfield, Virginia

Batik, Angelina, rickrack, hand-dyed trim, colored pencils, paint; drawing, machine-quilted.

Diane has loved the Beatles since she was a little girl. She remembers when they first performed on *The Ed Sullivan Show* one Sunday night. Her brother, Dan, was also a huge fan; he was always listening to their songs. When she was young, Diane sang in the choir and played the piano. She majored in art in college, where she was required to take art, music, and theater. Diane now listens to soft rock and oldies. She plays music all the time: in the car, at work, and when she's crafting. She says music helps her to clear her mind so she can let the creative juices flow.

Diane chose the song "Eight Days a Week" for this challenge because she thought it would be an interesting quilt to make. Since the song is all about love, she used a lot of hearts on the quilt to symbolize love. Everything is also done in "eights"; for example, there are eight hearts in the background. She loves doing art quilt challenges, Diane

professes, because they make her stretch her skills and really think about what to do as opposed to just using a pattern.

Diane has been sewing since she was a little girl. She took a "Stretch and Sew" class while she was in high school. Her mother is a great seamstress and was a big influence on Diane, always encouraging her to learn new things. Diane belongs to a group of six friends who work on art quilts. They have taken classes together and have learned from one another. She has been making art quilts for about five years. She says she quilts because "it's relaxing" and she loves "the color and feel of fabric." She is proud to have made a quilt for Jamestown's 400th anniversary; it was exhibited at the Virginia Quilt Museum.

Diane owns the Virginia Stained Glass Company, a retail store. She says working with stained glass is very similar to quilting because you "start out big, cut it up small, and then make it big again."

Cotton fabric, batik; fusible appliquéd, machine-quilted.

Linda has been a Beatles fan forever — she loves to hear their lovely melodies and believes their music goes with everything. She admits that the idea of creating a quilt using a Beatles song title was something "I could not resist" and, when she read the lyrics to "Eleanor Rigby," she could easily imagine the quilt she might make. She likes to challenge herself to use new techniques and tools to create quilts, and this one is a combination of what she has learned in art classes.

Linda's mom always made her clothes when she was growing up, so learning to sew was as natural as learning to cook. Her grandmother and aunts made quilts, too. They lived on farms in East Texas, where quilting was a tradition. The quilting frames hung from eye hooks and pulleys on the ceiling. After dinner, the table would be moved out and the large quilt frame could be carefully lowered to chair level. The women would each pull up a chair and quilt for a while. The only sewing machines they had were the treadle type, but most of the quilts were made entirely by hand,

using feed sacks as fabric. Linda cherishes a quilt she owns that was made in 1905. She also has a quilt that was handmade by her grandmother in the 1930s, which is the grandmother's flower garden pattern.

Linda made her first quilt in 1986 when the *Quilt in A Day* books were first published. Like the books promised, the quilt, a standard log cabin quilt, was made in a day. However, her second quilt — a double Irish chain pattern for a king-sized bed — was made "in more of a biblical day," she jokes.

Linda says she has enjoyed growing as a quilter over the past several years. She loves fabric: touching it, working with it, creating with it. She also likes that other quilters have their own unique technique. Her favorite art quilt subjects are fish. She and her husband do a lot of scuba diving and get to see beautiful aquatic creatures up-close, she enthuses. She has made several unique pieces featuring ocean life and wants to continue to explore ways to create more beautiful art quilts of this type.

"EVERY LITTLE THING"

Tom Anderson • Fairfax, Virginia

Cotton fabric, fusible webbing, charms; machine-pieced, raw edge appliquéd, hand-embellished.

Tom became a fan of the Beatles when he was a teenager. He remembers sitting around with his friends, just listening to the Beatles' records together. Today, he enjoys listening to country, rock and roll, and symphonies. He finds music to be soothing, inspirational, and therapeutic. "It relaxes me so I can think clearly," he says. He was in concert band, symphonic band, and marching band in high school. Now, he just "picks on" the piano and the banjo.

Tom shares that he selected the song "Every Little Thing" because it expresses how he feels about his wife, Judy, and their life together. His love for his wife inspired this quilt — his first quilt. He heard about the challenge from Judy and thought it sounded like fun. He recently retired from his career as an engineer and decided to jump in, feet first. The other thing that happened in the process of making this quilt is "Judy allowed me to use her new sewing machine!" Now, the couple need to rearrange the sewing room to be able to accommodate two people.

Tom confesses that he had been interested in quilting for a couple of years, as he wanted to transform pictures into fabric. He is in the process of investigating all aspects of quilting and has joined a local guild. He also enjoys walking the dog, boating, car repair, gardening, and biking. In order to complete this quilt in three weeks, he put cutting the grass on hold.

55

"EVERYBODY HAS SOMETHING TO HIDE EXCEPT ME AND MY MONKEY"

Jane LaGree Allingham • Fairfax, Virginia

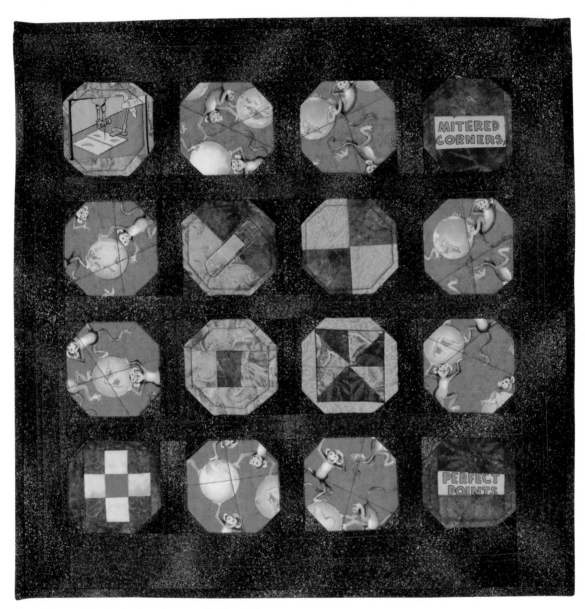

Cotton fabric, tulle, a band-aid; machine-pieced and quilted.

Jane considers herself a Beatles fan only because she is old enough to remember their music when it first played on the radio. Now she likes indie rock and acoustic music; she can't imagine her life without it. She plays the keyboard and hand drums. As for the effect music has on her creative process? Jane suggests fabric is a visual rhythm and music is an aural one.

She chose this song just because she wanted to use her monkey fabric, Jane explains. She chuckles that all quilters have something to hide and that is the story behind her quilt. Most viewers of quilts are quilters, so her quilt has a variety of things "behind the layer of tulle that quilters hide and quilt viewers look for." These things include points that don't match, the pinwheel that doesn't spin, the pucker, the thread that isn't clipped, blood from getting pricked by a pin or a needle (hence the band aid), and colors that run.

Jane began sewing years ago and her troll dolls were graced with her first sewing machine-made garments. Although she used to practice law, Jane now surrounds herself with fabric by working in a quilt store.

Cotton fabrics, crushed velour, various yarn, threads, and novelty embellishments; raw edge machine appliquéd and quilted.

Mari proclaims she is "chronologically old enough" to be a Beatles fan from the beginning. Music is in her soul and it is a major part of her identity. She was a flute major in college and played some piano, too; in fact, she is currently learning to play "Something" and "Let it Be." She enjoys listening to Broadway tunes, vocal and instrumental jazz, classical, adult contemporary, and, "of course, Josh Groban and the Beatles!"

Mari selected "Fixing A Hole" because it was the only one of the remaining songs that she knew, she explains. She collects novelty fabric with cats, dogs, and musical themes, so it was only natural that she would use some of her stash to make this quilt.

The August 5th deadline was fast approaching, and Mari knew she would need to work on her quilt until practically the last minute. To complicate matters, she had to go out of state the weekend before and was scheduled to return on the quilt's due date. On "Deadline Monday," she began her trip back to Virginia. Her husband drove

while she worked on the binding. What is usually a five-and-a half hour trip ended up taking longer because of an unexpected stop at a restaurant to have dinner with her son. While her husband and son ate, Mari continued sewing on the binding. She was only able to eat a couple of bites; her son took a picture of her sewing at the restaurant. Once back on the road, she continued to work through the highway construction and finally ended up delivering her quilt at 8:45 p.m. She apologized for turning in her quilt so late, but found out that about ten more quilts were still expected later that night. Mari was so relieved not to be the last one. As she left, two other vehicles pulled up in the driveway. A woman got out of her car, looking around because she was unsure which one was the right house. Mari asked, "Beatles quilt? You are at the correct house." The woman said her friend was still in the car, working on the quilt sleeve, under the car's dome light!

Mari smiled. "We quilters can so relate to one another!" she laughed.

"FOOL ON THE HILL"

Dolly Krach • Gainesville, Virginia

Cotton fabric, beads, bells, Swarovski crystals, hand-appliquéd, machine-stitched and quilted. Special thanks to Dolly's daughter, Denise M. Fayle, who did the original drawing of this design.

Dolly's daughters were always avid Beatles fans. One Sunday, the Krach family drove through Washington, D.C., on their way home from visiting relatives. The movie *Help* had just been released and was playing in one of the theaters there. Her husband surprised them and treated the family to a showing. Their girls were so excited; they still talk about it to this day.

This is Dolly's first art quilt. Her daughter, Denise, inspired her to create a quilt based upon "Fool on the Hill." Dolly says she isn't an artist and could not have done this quilt without Denise's help. Her typical style of quilting is traditional; this quilt enabled her to branch out and try her hand at appliqué. In the end, she admitted she spent way too much time on this little quilt. "I just became addicted to working on it!" she laughs.

Dolly says she has been "sewing forever," as her mother was a professional seamstress. Dolly was a bookkeeper at one time and took up quilting because she remembers always being fascinated with quilts. Nowadays, she claims, she would be lost if she didn't quilt. She also enjoys crossword puzzles, gardening, reading, and traveling.

Ann Littleton • Stafford, Virginia

Various blue fabric, assorted threads and fibers, buttons, beads, and other types of embellishments; machine-pieced and quilted. Special note: There is a tab that lifts toward the bottom of the quilt to reveal a QR code. When a smartphone scans the code, the song "For You Blue" plays.

Ann has enjoyed the Beatles music for many years. She remembers going to her neighbor's house to watch *The Ed Sullivan Show* when the group made their first appearance. She and her best friend, Kathy, danced in their sock feet to many of their albums during sleep-overs at each other's houses. They washed their hair and set it with big metal curlers with nylon bristles and put on huge plastic hooded hair dryers with hoses dangling, and then they dabbed their pimples with cream and danced away. Ann laughs at the memory now, saying "we must have been a sight!"

Due to her husband's Naval career, he was deployed for months at a time. Ann mostly stayed at home to raise "somewhat well-adjusted kids." With schooling in elementary education and speech pathology, she held several part-time jobs, including substitute teaching, decorating Christmas trees in a store in Freeport, Maine, and working at the Bowdoin College Library. She has also held many volunteer positions. She and her husband, whom she calls "Mr. Wonderful," recently celebrated their 41st anniversary.

Ann chose "For You Blue" because her son and his wife recently moved far away and she has been missing them. She listened to the song over and over again while making this quilt.

Ann began designing quilts in 1986; articles and photographs of her quilts have appeared in various publications, including on the cover of *Quilter's Newsletter Magazine*, and several of her quilts have been featured in nationwide exhibits. She is an experienced teacher and speaker who enjoys the topics of vintage design and embellishment, along with stories of the friendships of women in her quilts, trunk shows, workshops, and patterns. Proceeds go to help support Younglife and Hope Tree Children's Home in Salem, Virginia.

"FREE AS A BIRD"

Dottie Dane • Annandale, Virginia

Cotton fabrics; hand-appliquéd using Rose Han's method, machine-quilted. The bird design was adapted from Award-Winning Appliqué Birds *by Pamela Humphries.*

For Dottie, music has been a calming influence in her life. She mostly listens to classical, blue grass, folk, and oldies. She has been sewing for sixty-five years, beginning at the age of ten with a patchwork quilt for a doll bed. She used her mother's sewing machine to sew clothes, which her mother even "allowed me to wear to school!" Dottie majored in textiles and clothing at Cornell University. She designed and made her wedding dress, taught sewing classes, and managed a fabric store in Washington, D.C.

Dottie says she quilts because she likes to create with color and texture — and she loves the people she has met in the quilting world.

She chose the cardinal for this Beatles quilt challenge because her husband has a background in ornithology and they have many bird feeders in their yard. She loves the bright red birds that nest in the yard or sit on the snow-covered bushes in the winter and grace the feeders all year. She chose the appliqué technique for this quilt because it is one of her favorite methods of sewing. It is portable and she can sew while waiting or riding in the car. Dottie adds that she loves participating in challenges for the opportunity to stretch and grow as a quilter.

Dottie has been a real estate agent for over thirty years, and was also a professional Girl Scout recruiting and training leader for four years.

Mary Kerr • Woodbridge, Virginia

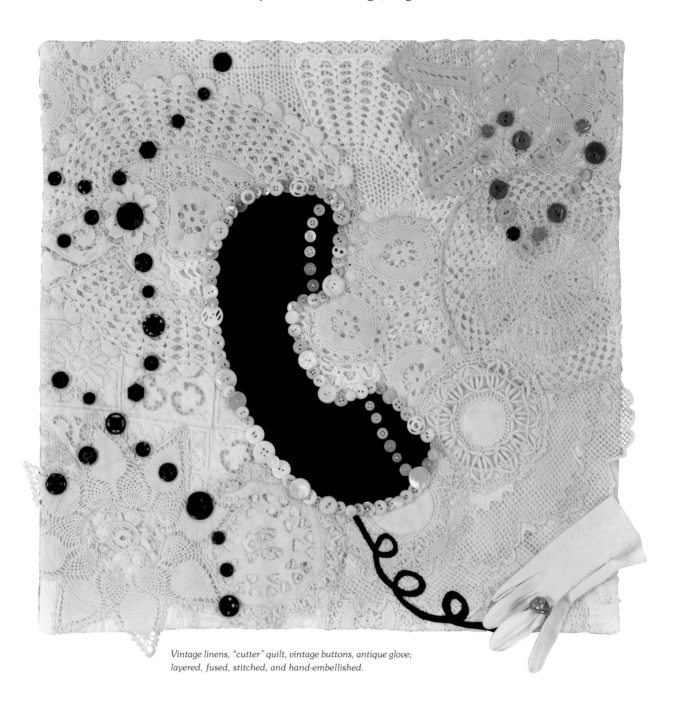

Vintage linens, "cutter" quilt, vintage buttons, antique glove;
layered, fused, stitched, and hand-embellished.

Although Mary appreciates the work of the Beatles, it isn't the music she grew up with. Her husband tells stories of the Beatles. He was the fifth of seven children and grew up listening to the great music of the '60s blasting from the bedrooms of his older siblings.

Mary asked her husband to choose the song for this challenge, since he was the Beatles fan, but vetoed his first choice, "Why Don't We Do It in the Road." What inspired the quilt she made were the words to the song "From Me to You." She says the lyrics were perfect for her and her husband of thirty-one years. The style of this quilt is typical of her work: layering vintage with strong silhouettes.

Music is a huge part of Mary's life. She grew up in a bluegrass tradition — almost all of her family events featured jam sessions, good fellowship, and lots of food — and she continues this custom with her own children and current circle of friends. Music Night at the Kerr's is an ongoing tradition. She sews with music playing in the background and reveals that her creative process is often influenced by lyrics or special song titles.

Mary grew up surrounded with quilts; all of the women in her family quilted. Her own work evolved into the art quilt form just over the past few years. She firmly believes we "can express

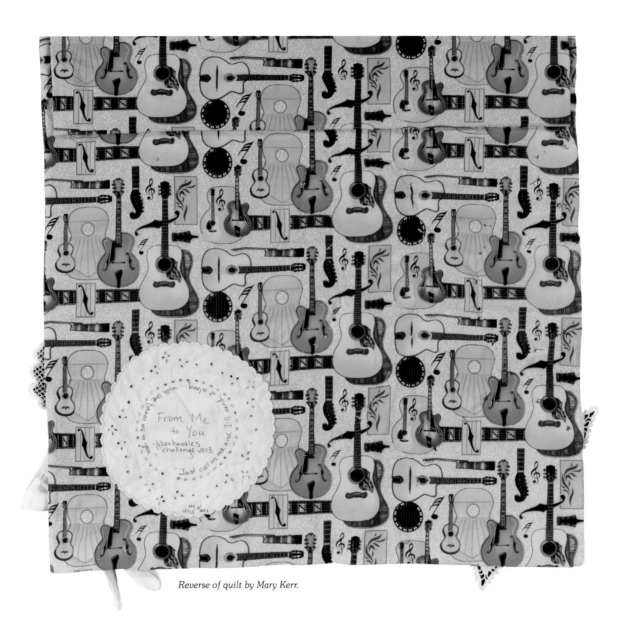

Reverse of quilt by Mary Kerr.

ourselves in many different ways in this medium." Some of her work is traditional and some could be called art, but most of her pieces are a combination of the two. All of her work incorporates vintage textiles of some kind.

Mary received her degree in social gerontology and she worked as a social worker before her children were born. She was an army wife and a stay-at-home mom who "never really stayed at home."

Mary creates for the folk art circuits, teaches quilting, and sells her work, patterns, and writings. She is also an American Quilt Society-certified appraiser and an award-winning quilter. She is a quilt historian whose lectures and workshops focus quilt history and the preservation of antique textiles. Her current work marries her love of all things vintage with the freedom of expression that is encouraged in the art quilt community.

As an accomplished author of art quilt books, next on Mary's to-do list is to continue work on a series of quilts for her next book, *Through the Garden Path*. This book will feature contemporary quilts created to show vintage hexagon pieces, tops, and fragments.

Lisa Holk • Overland Park, Kansas

Cotton fabric, faux fur; machine-pieced, appliquéd, and quilted, hand-appliquéd.

Lisa has always liked the Beatles, but not as much as her husband. She wanted this quilt to be something he could enjoy as much as she enjoyed making it, from the initial design to the finished product. She is too young to have witnessed Beatlemania in person and is only familiar with the videos she has seen online.

Lisa says music inspires her and creates a great atmosphere. She has been sewing for only about two years, though she grew up watching her mom quilt; her mom taught her most of her skills and brought her along to a Kansas City Modern Quilt Guild meeting. While there, fabric was handed out and a challenge was issued for everyone to make a quilt using all solids. Lisa used that fabric to make her first quilt.

Lisa let her husband select the song — he chose "Get Back" — because, she explains, not only was he more familiar with the Beatles, but having him choose the song was a way to include him in the challenge. She did a lot of research about this song. The Beatles sang "Get Back" multiple times during their rooftop concert in London in 1969. It was the last song they sang before the police broke up the performance, which was their last live performance. Lisa researched their guitars and what the group was wearing during the performance; she tried to capture the small details in her design.

This is Lisa's first art quilt. She considers herself a "modern quilter" who enjoys working without a pattern. She went out of her comfort zone to make this quilt, as she incorporated many new techniques she hadn't tried before.

A labor and delivery nurse, Lisa says she quilts because she loves starting with beautiful fabric and turning it into a beautiful quilt. She also enjoys making quilts for others and knows it's the most special gift she can give.

"GIRL"

Debra Woodworth Godwin • Fairfax, Virginia

Debra is a Beatles fan who appreciates the huge contribution they made to the development of rock and roll. She first became aware of the Beatles when she was in the sixth grade. Students who were much more sophisticated than her introduced Beatlemania to her class: music, haircuts, and clothing. Everything British was suddenly cool. They spoke in fake British accents, quizzed each other on lyrics, and competed to be the first to purchase the newest record. Debra's mother was not enamored with the Beatles, so Debra secretly listened to the tunes of their *Rubber Soul* album on her transistor radio late into the night under the covers. She recalls being lulled to sleep by "Norwegian Wood," "Girl," and "Michelle."

Debra muses that music serves to alter her moods now, lifting or calming as the circumstances dictate. It keeps her company while she quilts and lulls her to sleep at night. She can't imagine life without music. She currently has an eclectic taste in the types of music she enjoys, from Gregorian chants to Irish folk, pop, rock and roll, and emo. Music allows her to directly access her emotions without filtering through the cognitive process.

Debra thinks she may have been born with a needle in her hand. She has been sewing for as long as she can remember, and has always been drawn to fabric and the process of sewing and creating with cloth. She discovered quilting while in college.

Cotton fabric, embroidery floss; hand-embroidered, machine-quilted, piped binding.

Debra enjoys participating in art quilt challenges because they stretch her skills. "Girl" was chosen because it is her all-time favorite Beatles song. Memories flooded back as she listened to the song over and over again for inspiration, and the pending birth of the royal baby added additional vision. The quilt is her own design, and it's also her first hand-embroidered quilt.

As a child therapist, Debra uses creative mediums to help children express their feelings, learn about themselves and their world, and cope in their own unique way. She has used quilting in therapy sessions to help children process past emotional wounds and move toward healing. She gives away most of the quilts she makes — this quilter's house has no quilts! — to family and friends, as well as charity and comfort programs such as Quilts of Valor, Project Linus, and other community agencies.

Quilting is Debra's therapy. It calms her soul by occupying her body while she meditates and prays. While she quilts for others, she prays for their well-being. She always includes a Bible verse that pertains to the quilt or the recipient on the quilt label.

"GLAD ALL OVER"

Eileen S. Linares • Charles Town, West Virginia

Although Eileen doesn't consider herself a Beatles fan, she enjoys their music. By the time she was a teenager, the Beatles were hot. She enjoyed their music, but mostly listened to country and bluegrass. Recently, her daughter has started listening to the Beatles. Hearing their music waft from her daughter's room makes "me feel like a kid again."

Eileen comes from a very large and creative family. Growing up, they were quite involved in the Irish culture. They all did Irish dancing. Music was very much a part of her childhood. She grew up with five sisters and four brothers and they only had a ten-inch TV, so watching it was difficult. Music was something they could all share, no matter how many of them were in the house. They had a record player and speakers in the family room and it was not uncommon to have the music on loud enough to be heard throughout the entire house. Her mom played the harp, her brother the bagpipes, and her sister the hammered dulcimer. Though they frequently all played together, she recalls, the funny thing was that none of them could sing.

Eileen's mom was a seamstress and made all of the clothes for herself, their daddy, and all ten children; she continued to sew all of her own clothes, as well as clothes and gifts for her children and twenty-eight grandchildren, until a stroke disabled her a year-and-a-half before her death at the age of eighty-four.

Eileen began sewing when she was six years old. She and her mom picked out fabric and a simple pattern. She spent three weeks working on her skirt. It had buttons down the front and the fabric was red with blue and yellow flowers. She was so proud of that skirt; the first time she wore it was on an "out of uniform day" at school. She remembers being sad when someone asked her "if I was wearing one of my sisters' hand-me-downs."

The first quilt Eileen made was a wedding gift for her first husband in 1992. Though she had plenty of sewing experience, she had never made a quilt. She went to a fabric store, armed with the knowledge that she could make anything as long as she had a pattern. She selected a pattern and chose all of the fabrics that she would need and then proceeded to cut out the pieces for the queen-sized Victoriana Star quilt with scissors. She didn't know anything about quilting, rotary cutters, or cutting mats at the time.

When her daughter entered middle school, Eileen became a full-time mom. That's when she joined a local quilting guild — and a quilter was born. From that time on, she has spent her free time making quilts for her loved ones and decorating her home with her creations.

Eileen chose the song "Glad All Over" because "an idea popped into my head quickly, almost as if to say 'pick me, pick me.'" She was

Cotton fabric, flannel, buttons, ribbon, googly eyes; fusible machine appliquéd, machine-pieced and quilted, hand-embellished.

going through a very difficult time in her life and just the thought of being "Glad All Over" was appealing, she explains. In constructing this little quilt, she fused the words onto the background and then added the buttons and other embellishments. She put a layer of tulle on top of everything and then machine-quilted it to hold it all in place.

Eileen likes to cook and knit and she still makes clothes on occasion, but quilting is her true love. It is her way of relaxing and de-stressing. She doesn't know what she would do if she were unable to quilt anymore, but she knows her life would be a lot less colorful. She has enjoyed trying all different techniques, but she prefers the traditional styles. She likes hand-appliqué, but she also machine quilts for the sake of doing something faster. Her favorite block is the log cabin, and she says she challenges herself to "see the different looks I can get" from that one block, by changing the placement of colors and moving the blocks in various directions. She has made many quilts using the log cabin block and is still not bored with its possibilities.

"GLASS ONION"

Susan M. Bynum • Springfield, Virginia

Batiks, muslin, various threads, fusible web; raw edge appliquéd and free motion quilted.

Sue is "absolutely a Beatles fan!" Although she doesn't specifically recall this, she has been told by her brother that she saw the Beatles debut on *The Ed Sullivan Show* and actually started screaming with all of the girls on TV. Her parents and her brother, who was six at the time, were flabbergasted.

Because there are two musicians in her family, Sue listens to all genres of music: from classical to the classics of rock and roll, pop, jazz, fusion, dub step, to electronica. Her husband plays the drums and her son plays guitar. On occasion, she is treated to live music at home while sewing. She likes songs she can sing along to, much to her son's horror. What she listens to while she sews depends on her mood and the type of sewing she is doing. Hard rock is okay if she is just doing mindless piecing, but if she needs to think about the design or figure out mathematical details, she prefers instrumental music. When she is machine quilting, she likes to listen to songs that help her get a good rhythm going.

Sue's mother-in-law bought Sue her first sewing machine as a Christmas gift. Though she sewed as a child, she had gotten away from it for several years and started out making curtains, doorstops, pillows, and tablecloths. Eventually, she bought a book on how to make quilts. Her first song selection for this art quilt challenge was "And Your Bird Can Sing." Someone else participating in the project really wanted to do that song, so "luckily," Sue says, she gave it away. She then chose "Glass Onion" because not only is it an awesome song, but it would challenge her to do something she has never tried before. She listened to the song over and over again for inspiration while designing this quilt, and she gives special thanks to her son, Jeff, for his help with color and fabric selection.

"GOLDEN SLUMBERS"

Anne Smyers • Reston, Virginia

Cotton fabric, fusible web, oil paint sticks; photo transferred, machine-appliquéd and quilted.

Anne is a Beatles fan who knows who wrote every song, who sang the lead, what album it was on, and what era it's from. She also enjoys folk-rock, oldies, and some contemporary stuff by way of her twenty-something daughter, but left to her own devices she reverts to the music of her youth: James Taylor, Jackson Browne, Pete Seeger, Bob Dylan, Crosby Stills Nash and Young, and Paul Simon.

Anne says it would be hard for her to imagine life without music. Music stirs the soul, and she often finds songs to be evocative of other times in her life. Hearing certain songs takes her right back to when and where she was when the song was popular.

A quilting class at G Street Fabrics infected Anne with the quilting bug. After that initial class, she reveals, she decided to replace the artwork on her living room wall with an original fiber piece. A year later, she joined an art quilt class — and there has been no looking back.

Right before hearing about this challenge, Anne had been on a Beatles jag. She doesn't know what precipitated it, but "I started reading obsessively about them and listening much more critically to their music," she reveals. She read several books about the Beatles: biographies, overviews, pieces by their producers and engineers. This challenge thrilled her, she confesses, because she felt so inspired by the chance to interpret one of their songs visually.

Anne chose "Golden Slumbers" because of the image the song evoked. She wanted to portray a dreamlike vision and had the idea of a child's slumber—sound, safe, and peaceful. The young girl's sleep is deep and enveloping, in warm, magical layers. Wisps and tendrils of dreamy images float around the margins. The fairies and the enchanted garden of oversized flowers represent the magical elements of her dreams, where everything is possible and wondrous things happen. Anne used the only picture she has of her daughter as a sleeping child, and it turned out to be the perfect image for the quilt. While working on this quilt, the sleeping girl pictured on it "graduated from college," she proudly announces.

Elly Dyson • Annandale, Virginia

Cottons, blends, beads, and various embellishments; hand-pieced and appliquéd, machine-pieced and quilted.

In 1957, Elly graduated from college and married a West Pointer who was born and raised in Hawaii. At that time, she liked the Kingston Trio, the Hawaiian music of Kui Lee and Don Ho, Elvis Presley's gospel melodies and his other songs (complete with gyrations), gypsy and bohemian rhythms, and samba music from Rio. She grew up with her grandmother, who sang Irish tunes. She also listened to big band music from New York City and patriotic marches in parades. She learned to play the piano as a child, played in a WMCA drum and bugle group, and ended up as the first flute in the Bayside High School Concert Band and Orchestra. Today, Elly likes old show tunes, easy listening, big bands of years' past, Latin American music, church hymns, and Beatles songs.

Elly started quilting in 1980, after her mother-in-law gave her an appliquéd Hawaiian flag quilt to complete. Elly used dental floss to quilt the first two rows and then decided to take a class. She chose "Good Day Sunshine" because she looks forward to good days for herself and her husband. "We have both suffered from long illnesses recently," she explains.

Elly rarely works on one quilt at a time; she generally has five or six quilts in progress. Some works need time to gel and some quilts take years to find a final finish. She tries to do something quilt-related everyday, but her main endeavor is to get back all of her physical abilities after spending ten months in hospitals and rehab facilities. Due to illness, she reveals, "I had to re-learn to talk, eat, breathe, bathe, dress, and walk."

"GOOD MORNING, GOOD MORNING"

Jane Frenke • Berkeley Springs, West Virginia

Cotton, dyed wool, silk, organza, paint; felted, painted, discharged, appliquéd, machine-pieced and quilted.

Jane is a Beatles fan who vividly remembers having her face up to the TV screen while watching *The Ed Sullivan Show*. Music is essential to her everyday work because "it's soothing and at the same time invigorating and inspiring." She enjoys classical music and has it on sometimes just as background white noise. On the other hand, there are times when "I turn the volume up and conduct the 'Ninth Symphony.'"

Jane has been sewing since she was a child. She was a hand-weaver and had bunches of hand-woven scraps "I just couldn't throw away," so she pieced them into "fabric" and made a big quilt out of them — that was the beginning. She has been quilting for family and friends ever since. She is now a fabric designer who creates unique and one-of-a-kind materials to work with.

The song "Good Morning, Good Morning" gave her a vivid image of "the spring, the view out my window, a cup of tea, and a bird singing," Jane describes. This quilt is about the sunrise and the promise of a new day.

Jane recently won "Best in Show" for large quilts in the West Virginia Quilt Show and she has been published in *Quilting Arts* and other magazines. Her work has also appeared in the U.S. State Department Art in Embassies Program. She is inspired by circular shapes and has made a series of award-winning sphere quilts. She has a busy schedule teaching, lecturing, and giving tours of her studio. She encourages other quilters "to make mistakes and to have an adventure."

Hand-dyed cotton, watercolor pencils, fake eyelashes, monofilament, assorted threads; hand-colored, machine-pieced, appliquéd, and quilted.

George was always Kathy's favorite Beatle because he was "soooooo cute." She watched the group perform on *The Ed Sullivan Show* as so many fans did in the '60s.

Kathy loves the creative process of quilting and has taken many classes to learn different techniques. Her mother suffered from Altzheimer's before she died, and Kathy made art quilts to raise money for a project begun by Ami Simms to support Altzheimer's research for a cure. She made nineteen little quilts for this effort that were auctioned on Simms' website, the Art Quilt Initiative. (For more information, visit www.alzquilts.org.)

Kathy chose the song "Good Night" after listening to it and reading the lyrics. Ironically, the first time she listened to it…. "It nearly put me to sleep," she confesses, "so I could imagine John singing this lullaby to his little son, Julian."

Kathy is a financial and computer-related Federal Government retiree. She enjoys taking photographs of nature in its simplest form and then modifying those pictures in different ways to get ideas for future art quilts. If she didn't quilt, she would hop in her car and drive to every state in the U.S., take pictures, see nature up-close, and collect memories of the sights she'd see and the people she'd meet.

Kathy belongs to an art quilt group that meets once a month, and has quilts published in Ranae Merrill's book *Simply Amazing Spirals* and Mary Kerr's *Dare to Dance: An Art Quilt Challenge*. In her spare time, she loves to attend her grandson's baseball games; she is his number one fan.

"GOT TO GET YOU INTO MY LIFE"

Bobbie Dewees • Springfield, Virginia

Bobbie came to the U.S. at about the same time the Beatles did. Her dad was a career army officer and she was born and raised in Germany. In high school in the early '70s, she discovered the Beatles and began to enjoy their music. "Let it Be" was the class song for her graduating class.

From the age of six, Bobbie danced ballet; classical music was and still is her life. She loved dancing, and her love of music remains. Whenever she is in the house or car, music is always playing. Listening to music is a large part of Bobbie's creative process. "It's like being on stage as a ballerina; I have the technique, I know the steps, and the music lets me be free," she describes.

Bobbie has a B.F.A. in photography from Arizona State University, but she put away the darkroom supplies when it was no longer fun. About four years ago, there was an ad from a local quilt shop for art quilt classes. Bobbie wasn't sure what to expect, but she was new to quilting and wanted to see what it was all about. She bought quilting books and collected fabrics for months before finally taking the plunge. Her first sampler quilt was a disaster because "I didn't know the secret of the quarter-inch seam — none of the squares were the same size and I lobbed off points and corners by the dozens," she recalls. That first attempt became her dog's favorite blanket and it was buried with him when he died.

Cotton fabric, assorted beads, sequins, and permanent ink pens; drawing, writing, photo transferred, couched, beaded, machine-appliquéd, pieced, and embroidered.

When Bobbie read in an interview online that the "You" in "Got to Get You Into My Life" was marijuana, she was surprised, as she had always thought it was a love song. That is when "I decided to portray the 'pot-man' on my quilt," made up of a creative arrangement of terra-cotta planters. She describes herself as being "as square as the day is long" and says that is as close as she ever wants to get to marijuana!

Despite the music's actual meaning, Bobbie said she loved the sense of adventure she thought the song was about: being daring and going on adventures with no idea of what they might bring. The lyrics tell her to be brave and take chances and maybe, just maybe, love will really be found during the journey.

Bobbie had a blast participating in this challenge and is now convinced that, no matter what the outcome, she will enter more art quilt challenges. Bobbie is a single mother, cancer survivor, and a retired government employee. She has seen much of the world and is making the most of her retirement to be creative, read, belly dance, listen to music, and spend time with her son, who is her biggest supporter.

"HAPPINESS IS A WARM GUN"

Etta McFarland • Olive Branch, Mississippi

Cotton, silk, Timtex™, lace, tulle, beads, jewelry components, hot fix crystals, buttons, ribbon, shells, trims, glue; hand-appliquéd, cross-stitched, beaded, couched, machine-quilted.

Etta received her first phonograph when she was nine years old and the first records she got were by the Beatles: *Something New* and *The Beatles Second Album*. These are the only records she has held on to over the years. She listened to them over and over, imagining the Beatles coming to her town and hoping she would cross paths with Paul, who would recognize her as a kindred, though older spirit. Etta saw Paul in person when he came to Memphis in 2013. Unfortunately, their eyes did not meet, which is probably just as well since she was sitting next to her husband! However, she did enjoy the best concert ever: even in his seventies, he was non-stop energy, performing for over three hours straight. "I still love him," she professes.

In elementary school, Etta took accordion lessons, but the experience was short-lived when she panicked at the thought of playing in a recital. Performance anxiety did her in. In junior high school, she played French horn in the school band and continued until her junior year in high school. As much as she loves music, playing an instrument was not something she found fulfilling. She now listens mainly to classic rock and blues, although she also enjoys all rock and roll. She lives outside of Memphis, where there is an abundance of blues to be heard, from Beale Street all the way down the Mississippi Delta. There are several wonderful venues there for rock concerts and the Beale Street Music Fest is a weekend full of rock and blues bands. It is a great city for music lovers; music keeps her young at heart and her attitude positive.

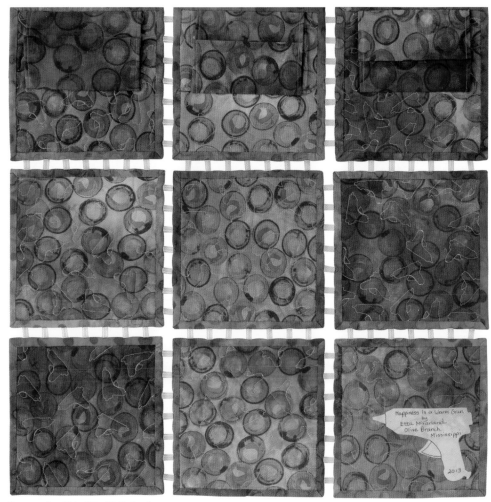

Reverse of quilt by Etta McFarland.

Etta loves listening to music when she is working on projects and often thinks of her pieces in terms of song titles. She used "Norwegian Wood," "Heart Like a Wheel," and "Fields of Gold" as titles for wearables.

Etta failed junior high home economics because she couldn't put the zipper into the right side of the skirt. She was convinced she would never sew. Necessity changed that when she was newly married and needed clothes to wear to work. She found great satisfaction in creating something she enjoyed wearing and that other people admired. Her first quilt was made from a pattern featured in a 1977 *Women's Day* magazine. "I saw the quilt on the cover and I was blown away," she declares. The next year, she took her first quilt class and was hooked. She quilts because "I love to be creative and I find a real kinship with other quilters." She was an air force wife for twenty-five years. Her family moved nearly every two years as she attempted to finish her journalism degree. She finally earned it at the age of thirty while she was pregnant with her second child. In all of her relocations, she first sought out the quilters and has always been welcomed with open arms. "Quilters are the best!" she exclaims.

Why did she participate in this challenge? "You had me at 'the Beatles,'" Etta laughs. She looked at the list of available songs and this one popped out. She knew instantly what she wanted to do and explains that she loves to add humor into her work whenever she can. How better to portray the joys of owning a glue gun than featuring beautiful projects made with one? She planned to make a "happy, fun quilt that is all about the glue."

Etta has competed in juried quilt shows, winning awards at both the local and national level. She is a nine-time participant in the Fairfield/Bernina fashion shows and was a top finalist several times. She won the "Crème de la Crème" award in the 2004 Bernina Fashion Show. In 2006, she won "Best of Show" and "Viewers' Choice" in the American Quilters' Society fashion show. Her work has been published in multiple magazines, including *Quilters Newsletter*, *American Quilter*, *Miniature Quilt Magazine*, *Quilting Arts*, *Quilt Almanac*, and *Sew News*. She was also the featured designer in the 2009 August/September issue of *Belle Armoire* magazine.

"HELP"

Beth Shafer • Fairfax, Virginia

Cotton, wool, chain, buttons, embroidery floss; appliquéd, machine-pieced, and quilted.

Beth still remembers laying in bed and listening to the Beatles first performance on *The Ed Sullivan Show*. She was only four at the time, but says she recalls thinking that she liked their music. The next day, she mentioned the Beatles to her mom who said they weren't very good and she didn't understand all of the fuss. Beth was shocked and decided to like them, anyway.

Depending on her mood, classical, bluegrass, rock and roll, steampunk, Christian, and Gregorian chants are what Beth enjoys. When she is doing something creative, if she needs to concentrate on a particular pattern, then classical and calm music is what she prefers. Otherwise, "it's usually something I can sing along with," she says.

This is Beth's first art quilt. When she thought of the song "Help," a complete quilt came to her mind. Of course, she adds, that is not quite how the final quilt turned out. We all need a little help at some point in our lives, sometimes professional, and at other times a friend will do. "This quilt shows how our fears have a ripple effect that reaches out to affect other aspects of our lives," Beth explains. The appliquéd fears are raw-edge, "as sometimes our troubles are not clearly defined." Only the couch and chair are needle-turned appliqué, so that they have clear borders. Bipolar disorder is represented by the circle with the two faces. (Beth gives special thanks to her brother-in-law, Andrew Gruchy, whose diplomas are shown on the quilt.)

Beth's degree was in mechanical engineering and now she is a substitute teacher. She quilts because "I love watching the patterns emerge from all of the separate pieces. There is satisfaction in creating something beautiful and useful." She gives most of her quilts away, she confesses, because "it is an added thrill to see other people enjoy what I have created."

"HER MAJESTY"

Ellie Flaherty • Falls Church, Virginia

Cottons and satin, various threads, ribbons, tulle, beads, Swarovski crystals and pearls, fusible web, Lutradur®, transfer artist paper, textile markers; fusible appliquéd, thread painted, beaded, hand-embroidered, machine-pieced and quilted. Special thanks to Ellie's brother, Mike, and niece, Emily, for taking photos of Max and Eubie. One of these was used to make the pattern for the Queen's Corgi.

In 1964, Ellie was a freshman in college in Boston, living at home and commuting to school. She watched the Beatles U.S. debut on *The Ed Sullivan Show* with her mom. They thought the Beatles were cute and fun, "but we couldn't imagine any guys wearing their hair that long," she laughs now. Her father thought they were disgusting.

In 1969, as a young bride, Ellie lived near an Air Force base in northern Texas while her husband was training. Any day might mean he could be sent to Vietnam. They were miserable and homesick. Ellie was working as an RN at the local hospital and she has vivid memories of ironing her white uniform in their tiny apartment while listening to *Abbey Road*, which had been released a few months earlier. She felt like that album somehow "kept me connected to the larger world." A year later, in 1970, their first son was born; they sang "Here Comes the Sun" to him. "He brought happiness and joy to an otherwise difficult time," she explains.

Fast-forward to 2013: the Flahertys have been married for forty-five years and they have raised four kids, all of whom play musical instruments. Ellie is retired from a forty-four-year career and now belongs to a fifty-five-years and over chorale. Their biggest crowd pleaser is "When I'm Sixty-Four."

Music plays a huge role in Ellie's life. She played the flute for several years and was in her college marching band. She tried her hand at the hammered dulcimer for a

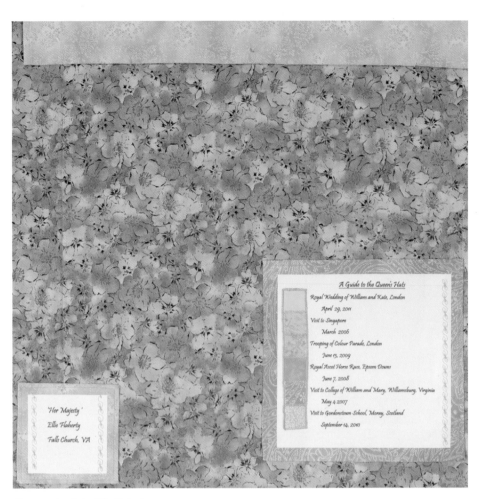

Reverse of quilt by Ellie Flaherty.

few years and has added "singing in a doo-wop backup trio" to her bucket list. She rarely has music playing in the background because she almost always has a song playing in her brain and they compete.

Ellie took a sewing class the summer before fourth grade. It was an ambitious class: the girls made themselves sailor dresses; hers was turquoise blue with white trim. She thought she could make anything, after taking that class. Years later, in 2010, she enrolled in an art quilt study group. She had recently been on a trip to Ireland and wanted to capture the colors and feel of Ireland in a fiber piece. She hoped the class would show her where to begin the method, but she never thought that art quilting would become her passion. It did. "I love the process of coming up with a vision and working with fabric, thread, and beads to make it happen. Things change as the construction unfolds and that's half of the fun," she enthuses. Plus, she gets to use some of the materials she's been collecting nearly all her life.

Although "Her Majesty" isn't one of the Beatles biggest hits, Ellie had a mental picture of how she would interpret the song and was glad it was still available. It is a little twenty-three-second ditty Paul sings as a bonus song at the end of *Abbey Road*. The Queen is well-known for her hats, which are always changing, so Ellie thought it would be fun to replicate some of them and depict the Queen trying to decide on one to wear. On the Internet, she was able to view hundreds of photos of the Queen through the years wearing a vast number of hats.

As she conducted her research, Ellie says, she gained an appreciation for the unique role the Queen plays in Britain's relationship with the world. "For six decades, this woman has graciously been the face of her country: its sense of continuity, its place in history. Nothing compares to that in the United States, despite our current collection of living past presidents," Ellie says. Seeing images of the Queen over the past sixty years, with world leaders, tribal leaders, rock stars, movie stars, everyday people, and extraordinary people, in moments of joy and sorrow, Ellie felt like she got to know her through her wonderful hats and declares: "What a life! What stamina! What a woman!" Of course, the Queen does love her Corgis.

Ellie says that while the quilt was fun to work on, it was also challenging to capture the Queen without using an actual photo of her. She doesn't have any formal art training, so she learned how to draw a face from children's books. She had her granddaughter take her picture in the pose seen on the quilt, enlarged it, and used that as the basis for a pattern for the Queen.

While she was making the quilt, Ellie's chorale group traveled to France, where they gave a concert in a cathedral in Rouen and sang "America the Beautiful" at the American Cemetery and World War II Memorial at Omaha Beach in Normandy. "It was the experience of a lifetime!" Ellie exclaims.

"HERE COMES THE SUN"

Marsha F. White • Fairfax Station, Virginia

Cotton, assorted sheer fabric, beads, fusible web; pieced background, fused, machine-stitched, beaded, and hand-stitched.

The Beatles burst onto the American scene, and the beat of their music and the words pulled Marsha right in. She saw them on *The Ed Sullivan Show* in black and white. This was a very big deal as her parents would not have let her watch it if it had not been broadcast on such a mainstream variety show, one that they watched every Sunday evening. Her parents definitely did not like the girls screaming and fainting, or the music, but that made it all the more compelling to Marsha. She loved that music!

Marsha learned to play the flute in the fifth grade and played through her first year of college. Joining the marching band in her new high school was a way to quickly become a part of school life and make instant friends. There is nothing like being on the football field marching to the beat on a cold Kansas Friday night and cheering the football team to victory…or not. Today, she enjoys listening to classic and contemporary rock, classical, bluegrass, and jazz.

Marsha finds quilting is a means of "tapping into the previously unknown creative side of my brain." She joined in this challenge because she felt it was a fun way to express her love of this fabulous music, which had been a big part of her teenage and adult life, and to learn the creation stories of many of their songs. She chose "Here Comes the Sun" because she loves the title, the music, and the words. The music's imagery and lyrics were her original inspiration, but then she learned the back story of George's personal problems in 1969. It seems the business side of the music was zapping his creativity. One day, he played hooky and visited a friend. Inspired by being in that friend's garden, he wrote this song. The shades of gray on the quilt represent the gradations of depression: life's totally overwhelming moments. Whether intentionally seeking the help of a friend or a professional, or receiving a serendipitous act of the divine, the impact of a walk in the woods, taking in the beauty of a garden, receiving the warmth and light of the sun, or accepting love or a helping hand can illuminate the darkness.

"HERE, THERE, AND EVERYWHERE"

Angela Laperle Miller • Alexandria, Virginia

Cotton fabric; raw edge appliquéd, machine-pieced and free motion quilted. Special thanks to Angie's husband, Jack, who helped with the drawing of his hand.

When Angie first began listening to music on the radio, she wrote out the words to the songs she loved. One of them was "Strawberry Fields Forever." It reminded her of visiting her Aunt Evelyn's home in New York State, where they picked strawberries from her backyard and sprinkled them with sugar before topping them over cereal for breakfast. Those were sweet memories and her first introduction to the Beatles. She says

music "eases me into the creative zone," where time is stilled. It's also a mood changer and a memory maker. She enjoys listening to country, light rock, classic rock and roll, and modern classical.

Angie learned to sew in junior high school with help from her mom and made several pieces of clothing. One piece that she was very proud of, and wore often, was a green top with a rectangle mushroom

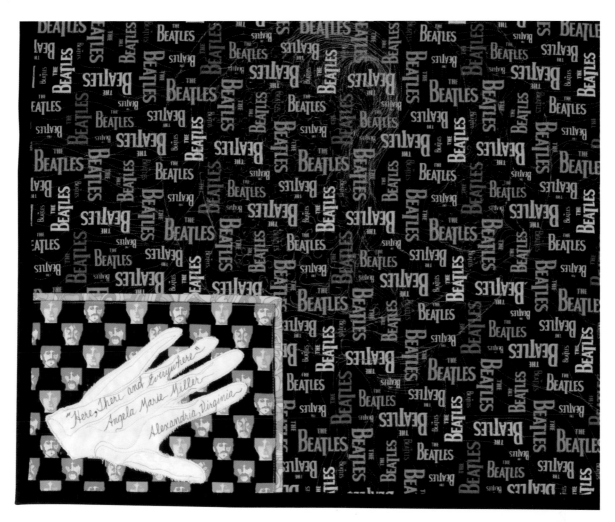

Reverse of quilt by Angela Miller.

print. Years later, when she had to get rid of the top, she cut out the rectangle and made it into a pincushion — her first creative project. She began quilting to make quilts for her nieces and nephews as they graduated from high school. Now she is trying to branch out and create some of the ideas floating around in her brain. She has been making art quilts for the past five years.

When this art challenge came up, Angie was surprised to discover how many songs the Beatles had written. Ultimately, she claims, "I am a hopeless romantic," which is why she chose "Here, There and Everywhere." She loves the idea of love: the energy and joy that fills the space around two people who care for each other and who think of the other first. Two phrases that refer to hands in this song served as her inspiration. Angie believes our hands play an important role in all kinds of relationships. "How strongly or gently we use our hands can, indeed, be life-changing, from how we use them with our work, to how we comfort those we love," she explains.

Angie referred to several books for technical approach while making this quilt. In the process, she realized she could blend some of one technique with another. She pulled ideas and inspiration from the quilting books *Serendipity Quilts*, *Color Shuffle*, and *Pieced Curves*. She stretched herself to make this quilt, both technically and creatively,

and says she is most proud that all of the materials she used, including the thread, were what she already had on hand.

While making this quilt, Angie's niece, Emily, had a beautiful summer wedding planned and the family all came together to share this special event. After an evening of celebrating, Julianna, one of Emily's cousins, walked from the reception across the street. As she approached the sidewalk's edge, pausing for traffic to pass, a car veered toward her. Julianna was struck and fell to the ground; the driver of the car continued driving, leaving behind a trail of glass and plastic. Julianna's hand was shattered, her wrist broken. It was her right hand, the one she used to create beautiful illustrations as a young artist. There was a long surgery performed the next day. Everyone was thankful she was alive.

During this time, Angie had been applying finishing touches to her quilt. While stitching over the image of her husband's hand, it "occurred to me that it was the hands of a driver without a conscience who caused Julianna's injury," she reveals. What an ironically tragic twist to how our lives can change with the wave of a hand.

The longer she lives, the more Angie glimpses connections that bring deeper meaning to life. "Those connections are all around us — here, there, and everywhere — each and every day," she exclaims.

"HEY BULLDOG"

Pat Washburn • Chantilly, Virginia

Cotton fabric, ribbon, embroidery thread; machine- and hand-quilted, embroidered, appliquéd.

Pat was in high school when the Beatles came to the U.S. for their appearance on *The Ed Sullivan Show*. Her parents and grandmother thought the mop hairstyles were outrageous. Pat and her friend went to the drugstore in her small Midwestern hometown and pined over magazines with the Beatles' pictures in them. She made a scrapbook of the Beatles' magazine articles; she was "truly in love with Paul," she gushes, and thought he was dreamy.

Pat says music can make her happy or sad. She listens to classical, jazz, and pop music from the '50s, '60s, and '70s. In the course of life as a military wife, Pat tended to hold on to things that were familiar to her. They moved twenty-three times in thirty years, all around the world, but she still has her Beatles' albums.

An art and photography teacher for thirty-two years, Pat started sewing and quilt-making in January 2013. She was invited to a Fairfax Quilters Unlimited meeting by her friend, Linda, and enjoyed the speakers and seeing all of the beautiful quilts that the members brought for show-and-tell.

Pat's husband got her a dog when they lived in Thailand sixteen years ago. They named him Nitnoy, which means "little bit" in Thai. Pat was homesick for the States and the dog filled a place in both of their hearts. When Nitnoy died a year ago, they got a new French bulldog puppy. She describes the Marquis De Lafayette as "a laugh a minute with his funny face and silly antics." Pat's daughter lovingly calls him her puppy brother.

When Pat saw the song title "Hey Bulldog," she knew this was the quilt she wanted to make. She listened to the song and did her best to photograph her dog. This was difficult because "he doesn't stay in one place for long," she explains. When she began to draw him, she tilted his head to show his playful, happy personality. She had to stitch at night because she was busy during the day in the summer with her granddaughter during "Granny Camp." Though it was a challenge to complete the quilt on time because she was so busy with travel and family, Pat says she's glad she participated. "The Beatles and their songs have always reminded me of a happy, playful time in my life," she explains.

Vivian Milholen • South Riding, Virginia

Cotton fabric, fusible webbing; appliquéd, satin stitched, free motion quilted.

Vivian has been a Beatles fan for many years. When she was a child, she saw their debut on *The Ed Sullivan Show*. As they were performing, the show did a cutaway of girls screaming and fainting when they saw the Beatles. Vivian was so confused by this that she ran and got her mom and made her watch. When she asked her mom why this was happening, her mom laughed and said, "They are just boy crazy. Someday you will understand!" Her mother was right, of course, Vivian says, adding that today "music makes me want to dance, cry, and contemplate life." She enjoys songs from the '60s and '70s, as well as contemporary Christian music. She took piano lessons in her youth and guitar lessons as an adult.

Vivian's mom was an excellent seamstress by profession, and let Vivian make doll clothes beginning when she was five years old. Years later, in 2003, a good friend introduced Vivian to art quilting. "I love the texture it creates," she exclaims, explaining that she quilts because "it soothes my soul."

"Hey Jude" has always been one of Vivian's favorite songs, and the quilt was inspired by the lyrics. Vivian typically makes landscapes, but this quilt took her in a new direction — "it brought out my wild side," she confesses. While working, she kept rearranging the pieces and wasn't happy with the "world." As she was removing the quilt top from the design wall, the "world" fell over on one of Jude's shoulders and that's where Vivian decided she liked it. Most of the work on this quilt was done in the wee hours of the morning, as Vivian was spending her days working on the Sacred Threads committee. Her daughter also got engaged, so time was very short.

Vivian is a member of Fiber Artists @ Loose Ends, Studio Art Quilt Associates, The Quilt Alliance, Quilt Monkeys, Fiber Artists for Hope, and the Surface Design Association. She leads a Prayers and Squares group at her church and helps collect food for the Loudoun Interfaith Relief.

When Julie and her sister came home from school everyday, the first thing they did was put on one of their Beatles albums and sing along. They copied the Beatles' signatures and collected Beatles bubble gum cards, which Julie still has. She still has her 45s, but doesn't have anything to play them on anymore. She has also seen Paul once in concert when he was with the group Wings. During the early 1980s, Julie's house was broken into. All of her Beatles albums were taken…and she was crushed. She told her boss about it and said she hoped to replace them at some point in the future. When Christmas rolled around later that year, her boss gave her all of the old Beatles albums he could find at the record store. "I was so stunned and speechless," she reveals, but she will never forget his kindness. She still has the albums. "They mean the world to me," she exclaims.

Julie continues to listen to the Beatles. She enjoys the older music she grew up with and likes big band music, too. The *Rod Stewart Song Book* albums are also favorites. She loved the first few years of the TV show *Glee* because a lot of that music was older. She still remembers the slow and beautiful version of "I Want to Hold Your Hand," which Kurt sang.

Julie started sewing in junior high school by making clothes for herself. Back then, everyone took home economics and learned to sew. When she was fourteen or fifteen, her mother put a quilt on her bed. It was

Wool felt, felted wool, and embroidery floss; hand-appliquéd.

red, yellow, and "poison" green. It was love at first sight and Julie vowed to learn to quilt. It was a star quilt, completely pieced and quilted by hand, made by her paternal grandmother. It was her grandmother's first quilt and had never been used. Her grandmother was a seamstress working in Washington, D.C., and she made clothes for politician's wives. Julie found all of this out when she asked her aunt about the quilt when she had it appraised. "It's amazing the things you learn when you ask," Julie shares.

Julie started quilting for herself in the early 1980s. Craft shows were popular then and she and a friend started a little craft business. She made baby quilts and doll quilts and saw this as an opportunity to practice. She then became more serious about quilting. "I took some classes and learned to hand quilt," she explains.

The song "Honey Don't" jumped out at her. "Honey" makes Julie think of primitive quilts. She had never made an orange quilt, or a quilt out of wool, using her own design. In the beginning of creating the quilt, she listened to the Beatles music. As she got further along, she just hummed "Honey Don't" while she sewed. "I enjoyed working on it and learning something new and different," she admits.

Like many quilters, Julie has countless number of half-finished projects to complete. After working in human resources for Washington, D.C., law firms for twenty years, she now works as a receptionist. She also worked part-time at the Jinny Beyer Studio, but recently retired. She misses the customers very much, but says she has a little more time for herself and to sew now. If she didn't sew, Julie concludes, "I would learn to cook."

"HONEY PIE"

Catherine S. Tyler • Bon Air, Virginia

Cathy is a Beatles fan. At the time they became popular, she didn't realize how much they reflected the changes happening in the '60s and early '70s. In the late '90s, she saw the Mahoney Brothers tribute show, where they followed the Beatles through the years with music and costumes. "It was like reliving those years on fast-forward," she reveals. The natural sense of humor and wonderful enjoyment of life the Beatles had continues to appeal to her.

Today, Cathy listens to the Beatles, rock and roll, blues, and jazz. "Music lifts my spirits," she says. She tried to learn multiple instruments, but has "no ear." Nevertheless, she is thrilled her husband and daughter are both musicians.

Cathy's mother and grandmother were both accomplished seamstresses. Cathy began to sew in high school. She started quilting in 1992 and found it much easier than fitting garments. She made her first landscape quilt in 1999 and loved the freedom and excitement of using traditional quilting techniques to create something new and different. For her, quilting is "a unique way to capture and share the tactile quality of fabrics and the rich palette they provide" while also keeping her calm.

Cathy participated in this challenge not only because she loves the Beatles, but also because she has great respect for another participant, Paula Golden, and her artistic ability. It was Paula who invited her to join this project, and Cathy chose "Honey Pie" because she loves honey and thought she could come up with a fun play on words.

Cotton fabric, yarn, paint sticks, ink; raw edge appliquéd, couched, embellished with paint sticks, hand-carved stamp accents.

As Cathy bounced ideas around with her design consultant (her husband), he suggested she use the symbol for pi. In researching pi, she came across the hexagon inside and outside of a circle, which is a stage in the approximation of the value of pi. Moving on from there, the hive/honeybee/pi design that appears in the quilt evolved. She wanted the edges of the cells to be a bit raised, like one sees in a honeycomb, so she couched yarn around them and she used various sizes of hexagons to give a feeling of depth. She cut a stamp from a carving block and printed a few on the quilt and used one as an appliqué. She made the quilt a large hexagon by couching off the corners and embellishing them with an oil paint stick over a honeycomb texture plate. She also used a hive-like quilting pattern.

Cathy didn't listen to the Beatles while she made the quilt, but she did listen to the entire Beatles collection as she drove nine hours back from vacation. While making the quilt, there was a lot of sadness in her life. There were two deaths of family members in their nineties and her brother-in-law was ill, so she appreciated having an interesting sewing challenge to dive into from time to time, and she is very eager to see what other participants came up with.

Cathy worked for over thirty years for the Federal Reserve Bank of Richmond, mostly in information technology and project management. If she didn't sew, "I would just find another excuse not to clean the house, like maybe take up master gardening or hike the Appalachian Trail," she laughs.

Susan Bagshaw • Reston, Virginia

Cotton fabric, fabric paints, markers, thread, embroidery floss, beads, buttons, art transfer paper; drawn, painted, stitched.

Susan was in the sixth grade when "I Want to Hold Your Hand" hit the airwaves, and that year she played the part of George Harrison in the school holiday extravaganza. She has loved the Beatles as a group and individually for much of her life. Her heart broke when John was murdered and she still mourns losing George. She sings the Beatles songs often, and also listens to mostly classic rock. Her favorite artists are Jimi Hendrix and Vincent van Gogh.

Susan signed up for the Beatles art quilt challenge because she wanted to participate in another bee challenge with her gang. She chose "I Am the Walrus" because it was one of the few remaining songs with an animal in the lyrics. Henri Rousseau's painting *The Dream* inspired this quilt. While constructing it, Susan started drawing and then painting the idea that grew in her mind. The image became more complex. She fell in love with it and

realized she wasn't willing to stitch on it or part with it, so she eventually made another one and then stitched and quilted it. She describes it as "a bit psychedelic" because of the colors and the way it is pieced together. "It's also very 1960s because of the patchwork," she enthuses.

Though Susan was previously vice president for an international consulting firm, her life has covered a wide and varied territory. She was a cook in a health food restaurant, worked in an accounting firm, and was a welder. She also managed technical support for a tax software product, taught accounting, sold hand-made puppets at craft fairs, worked as a bartender and at a bicycle shop, was a medical assistant, and an office clerk at London Fog Raincoats. She feels her current job in consulting is a good fit for her "because it is a constantly changing and challenging environment."

"I ME MINE"

Betsy Wells Stone • North Springfield, Virginia

Betsy first learned about harmony when she and her fifth-grade girlfriend sang "She Loves You." Betsy's note went down and her friend's note went up as they sang "oooooooo." It turned out to be quite a surprise. Betsy saw the Beatles live on *The Ed Sullivan Show* with her family and her older brother said, "You want to scream too, don't you?" She answered no, but she didn't mean it. She comes from a very proper Southern family, so she held back her true feelings of overwhelming enthusiasm. Her mother thought the Beatles' songs were terrible and had no musical value.

In 1969, Betsy, her mother, and her siblings were in the elevator heading to the dentist. Her older brother asked her mom if she liked the tune that was playing. She listened for a moment and then said she did. He then announced it was the Muzak® version of "Yesterday" by the Beatles. Her mother admitted it was a good tune. Betsy laughs as she remembers thinking, "Praise be to my brother!"

In high school in northern Virginia and at Bethany College in West Virginia, Betsy played the clarinet in the symphonic band and orchestra, the alto saxophone in the marching band, and the tenor saxophone in the jazz band. Now, she listens to rock and roll, folk, classical, country, jazz, blues, and show tunes. She likes to immerse herself in her albums or CDs, Betsy says, to get the

Cotton fabric, glass beads, yarn, and various decorative threads; appliquéd, machine-pieced and quilted, beaded, and thread painted.

"full effect of the musician's intent." This was first awakened by wearing headphones and listening to the Moody Blues' *To Our Children's Children's Children* album. What an intimate experience headphones brought to listening to music, she remembers feeling.

Betsy has been sewing for fifty-four years. Her grandmother gave her a needle and thread and taught her to sew doll clothes at the age of six. She learned cross-stitch and completed a sampler by the age of twelve. She also learned how to use a sewing machine and follow patterns. At the age of thirteen, she made a cocktail dress for her mother. She later made two prom dresses, two bridesmaid dresses, many of her high school clothes, plus three matching, all-in-one, bell bottom pantsuits in a lime green and pink paisley print for her little sister, her mother, and her thirteen-year-old self to wear to a family reunion. It was "far out!" Betsy laughs.

Betsy has been making art quilts for about three years. She has an on and off obsession with quilting. "I'll quilt furiously for a while and then take weeks or months off to do other activities," she explains.

She gets great satisfaction from completing projects, but she has four times as many projects in progress than completed projects.

George is her favorite Beatle, so when she was looking for a song to claim, she researched every one of his songs. She discovered "I Me Mine" was the very last song recorded under the Beatles' name. She also learned this song was a Hindu lesson, speaking against letting one's ego rule as the focus of life. The more she listened to the lyrics and researched the meaning of the song, George's life, and the Hindu religion, the more inspiration she received for the quilt. She also felt confirmation about George — the Beatle she had always gravitated towards did not disappoint.

In making this quilt, Betsy used as many colors and patterns as she could to create the psychedelic nature of the time during the Beatles' reign. The basic form of the quilt is the mandala, a Hindu spiritual and ritual symbol representing the universe. The center eye represents the "I" in "I Me Mine" while other details in the quilt contain symbols and various references to the Beatles' lives.

Lesly-Claire Greenberg • Fairfax, Virginia

Since 1963, Lesly-Claire has been swooning over Paul. When the Beatles were to appear on *The Ed Sullivan Show,* her family was snowed-in. Her friend Dara watched it with her on the TV in the basement because "my parents didn't want to hear the noise." Today, she enjoys country, folk, and some new age music for relaxation. She realized recently that she no longer listens to music; she listens to CDs of books — and many of her quilts have been influenced by the book she was listening to at the time and various stories produced different results.

Lesly-Claire's grandmother was a gifted seamstress and her father and grandfather worked in the menswear industry, so she has been surrounded by fabric and sewing all of her life. She took the standard home economics class as a seventh-grader and made a gathered skirt with a zipper. In the eighth grade, she learned to use a pattern and made a patchwork vest. In high school, she and her best friend, Lori, made many of their outfits.

Lesly-Claire has always made art quilts. She first took a design class taught by Michael James. The quilt she made using sketches from that class won show ribbons. She took another class by artist Nancy Crow and, in 1980, she co-founded "New Image Artists" for the purpose of creating quilts that would be accepted as art and hung in galleries. This group continues to thrive as a support and critique group. In her art quilts, Lesly-Claire doesn't try to make statements. "I just want to make something pleasing. If it pleases others as well, that is even better," she explains.

Lesly-Claire wanted to do this challenge because she loves the Beatles. She also wanted to be a part of what she believes will be a showstopper. She chose "I Saw Her Standing There" because it brought an image to mind; it also was not a cover song, written by someone other than the Beatles. The title and lyrics inspired her quilt, though the design sat untouched for a long time while she recovered from major surgery. When she was able to get around the house again, her husband poster-ized her two-inch drawing to twenty-four inches. She used Photoshop to re-size the image, "painted" a bit more, and had the fabric printed at Spoonflower. This is one of the first times she has used raw-edge appliqué and fusing in an exhibition piece, she admits, adding that she plans to use this method more often because "it allows me to be more spontaneous."

Cotton fabric, artist-designed commercially printed linen fabric, threads and fusible web; machine-pieced, fused, raw edge appliquéd.

"I WANT TO HOLD YOUR HAND"

Tina Lewis • Parker, Colorado

Cotton fabric printed by home computer; Photoshop® filtered, machine-quilted.

Tina has been sewing for a long time. She got her start because she had some Sunbonnet Sue blocks that her grandmother had made that her mom wanted her to use in a quilt. When she started quilting, she found she kept trying to tweak a pattern. She got tired of doing the same traditional quilts and was encouraged to take art quilting classes. She has been taking classes for eight years now and has come to realize that she just didn't know to call what she made "art quilts" in the beginning. Tina says she quilts because "I like to create and have something useful to show for the time I spend working on a project."

Tina believes in music therapy. When she is down, the right music "can elevate my mood." She chose "I Want to Hold Your Hand" for the Beatles art quilt challenge because she had a nice photo of her son and a friend holding hands.

The day after completing this quilt, Tina moved from northern Virginia to Colorado. She has found like-minded companionship among quilters there and has already started a brand new art quilt group. An upcoming project they have planned is to each make a small art piece inspired by favorite music.

As she awaits the builders who are completing her dream home, Tina is settling into a new lifestyle and says that Parker is a great town.

"I WILL"

Maggie Ward • Warrenton, Virginia

Maggie clearly remembers the winter the Beatles came to the U.S. for the first time. She was in junior high school: prime Beatlemania age. The tickets to the show were only about seven dollars each, but that was out of her price range, since her allowance was fifty cents a week. Her lucky friend Julie McConnell went to see the Beatles. She came to school the next day with three black hairs she swore she had pulled off of Paul's head as he ran by. They looked suspiciously like Julie McConnell's hair, though, Maggie fondly recalls.

Maggie learned to sew on her mother's Featherweight, making little doll blankets and later on sewing clothes. She thinks she was born to be a quilter, but she didn't start quilting seriously until 2005. Though she started out making traditional quilts, she yearned to do pictorial quilts and a couple of years ago, she discovered quilt artist Ruth McDowell, whose paper-piecing methods provided her with the means to make pictorial quilts.

A strong confluence of events led her to join this challenge, Maggie reports. Her son got engaged. In preparation for the wedding, they got the house painted. In preparation for painting, she cleaned out her closet, where she found her mother's wedding dress, as well as her own. She fretted over what to do with them. She had no immediate inspiration, so she put the dresses aside. Next, her son said he'd like their mother/son dance to be to "I Will," as they have always shared

Satin brocade, cotton voile, assorted commercial fabrics; machine-pieced and hand-quilted.

a love for the Beatles. Her son had a wonderful wedding and they danced to the song. A few days later, another quilter told her about this challenge. She decided to take the plunge if "I Will" was still available. Serendipitously, the song had been previously selected, but the original artist had just dropped out the day before for health reasons.

On a post-wedding high, Maggie connected "I Will" to the vows at the wedding. She decided to use the wedding dresses from her closet in the quilt. While making this quilt, she kept Pandora® (Internet Radio) tuned to the Beatles channel. She reconnected with her mother through the process of cutting up her wedding dress. "My mother passed away in 1995, but I could feel her with me as I cut and stitched," Maggie reveals. As she cut up her own dress, she remembered the joy they shared at her wedding and, for the hundredth time, she wished she and her mom could have shared quilting together. Maggie knows her mom would have been thrilled to have her dress used in a Beatles quilt inspired by her grandson's wedding. "Mom, when you bought me my first Beatles album in 1964, who knew the ripples that would cause?" she remembers thinking.

Kerry Faraone • Purcellville, Virginia

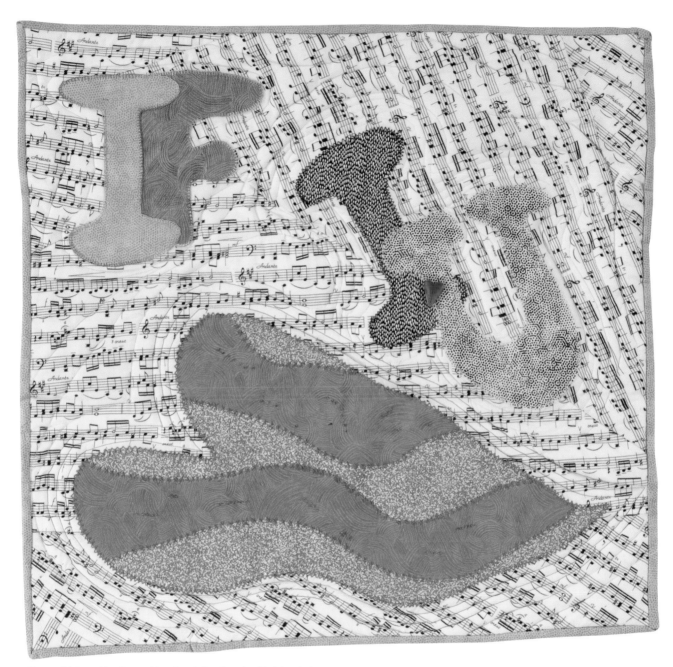

Cotton fabric and beads; machine-pieced, fused, and quilted, beaded.

Kerry has been a Beatles fan since their first appearance on *The Ed Sullivan Show*. She enjoys listening to all music. "Music can calm a busy mind and allow for creativity to begin," she comments, explaining the relaxing effect it has on her life.

Six years ago, Kerry's sister sent her a box of quilting books — that is how long she has been quilting. She began making art quilts when a group she's in decided to follow a lesson-by-lesson book.

When asked how she came to participate in this challenge, Kerry insists that "friends made her do it." She had a faux brother named Jeff who played the guitar and it was all Beatles music that he played. She chose "If I Fell" for her quilt because that song was their best harmony. This quilt is not her typical style, though, as she enjoys making quilts that are both contemporary and colorful. If she didn't quilt, she would do photography.

Kerry currently works as a shipping manager at a quilt shop. Next on her to-do list is to make a memorial art quilt.

"I'LL BE ON MY WAY"

Rosalie Phillips Lamanna • Alexandria, Virginia

Cotton and lamé fabric, various beads, pompoms, fiber and trim; paper-pieced, machine-pieced and quilted, appliquéd, hand-embellished and couched.

The Beatles obviously were tremendously creative talents who still draw fans young and old. Rosalie says to count her among the latter! Typically, she prefers soothing music and lyrics. For this challenge, she selected "I'll Be On My Way," a McCartney-Lennon collaboration recorded just once in 1963, but not released until 1994. She listened carefully to the lyrics and let them roll around in her head for several days; they were full of descriptive images.

Once it was time to get to work, what ensued was two weeks of concentrated effort as the quilt took over her life. Beginning with a large piece of paper to plan out the finished size, Rosalie started drawing ideas. Next came selecting the colors, material, thread, and embellishments to possibly include on the quilt; she used some of it and discarded some, all the while adding, subtracting, and modifying. Rosalie confesses that for her, the journey of making a piece is more fun than the finished product.

The fabric was pieced, paper-pieced, and assembled on the surface of the batting and then hand-stitched and quilted. The fun elements were added: the stuffed parts were appliquéd, the ribbon and beads were stitched in place, stars were put in the sky and fish in the river, and the pompoms became bushes.

Rosalie is grateful for these types of artistic challenges. "They spark my brain to get involved in a new creative endeavor and that's what puts the pizazz in life," she explains.

When creating, silence works best for Rosalie. Her brain cannot be out to lunch, busy with something else, or have other sensory input. She closely evaluates what she might deem at first to be a mistake because, in reality, it might be the best thing that could happen and just what the piece needed. She won't rush the process, but savors it… and then, she'll be on her way.

Julia Renken • Fairfax, Virginia

Cotton fabric, beads; machine-pieced and quilted, hand-embellished.

Julia has been a Beatles fan since 1964. She has never been to a Beatles performance, but she listened to many hours of Beatles music on Radio Caroline and Radio Luxembourg when she lived in The Netherlands in the late 1960s.

Today, Julia is partial to classic rock, 1990s country, and classical music. She says classic rock makes her quilt faster and helps her to create "happy" quilts, whereas classical music is better for traditional quilting. Her earliest memory of sewing is making doll clothes when she was in the third grade, when her mother taught her to hand sew. In home economics class in the seventh grade, she loved sewing, but hated cooking — and that hasn't changed over the years.

Julia says she was "talked into" doing the Beatles art quilt challenge. Her quilt, "I'll Cry Instead," depicts teardrops falling and creating splashes on the pavement. This is her first real art quilt and she confesses that, although doing it was a little outside of her comfort zone, it was fun to create.

Julia first sewed bedcovers. She then started quilting in order to make baby quilts for her daughters. The other reason she quilted was to provide companionship with friends overseas when she couldn't work. Quilting has supplied her with best friends and given her a wonderful creative outlet in semi-retirement from her job as a CPA. Now that every bed at her house has a quilt or two, she finds joy making quilts for others. Quilting is her way of giving back to her community.

"I'LL FOLLOW THE SUN"

Paula Golden • Blacksburg, Virginia

Paula enjoys listening to all kinds of music; her heart beats to rhythm. She identifies with ancient cultures and their chants with gourds and drums because it grounds her to the earth. Melodies bring her to tears or make her spirit soar.

When Paula was four years old, she wanted to play the harp, but the cost of the instrument was way out of her family's budget. Her parents suggested she learn how to play the piano, as it was the basis for most instruments. Her mother purchased a fifty-dollar upright vintage piano with pearl inlay that weighed "almost a ton...it took five men to move it," she recalls. She took piano lessons for seven years and then played percussion instruments (triangle, wood block, and Glockenspiel) in the elementary school orchestra. In the seventh grade, she learned how to play the clarinet and played in the high school band. A highlight was playing "Rhapsody in Blue" at the Palmengarten, Frankfurt, Germany. She also played folk guitar because that was a must for teenagers in the 1960s.

Today, Paula listens to music by Yanni to help her creative process. The analytical side of her brain keeps time with the rhythm and the creative side leads her to play with ideas, linking one to another. Her mother taught her how to cross-stitch when she was seven, but she wasn't very good at following the designs, especially when her mom said the back of the piece should look as beautiful as the front. She was glad when counted cross-stitch came along because then all of her little "x's" were the same size. She learned how to sew from her mother and made her own clothes as a teenager. She even made a wool dress, completely by hand.

Paula chose the song "I'll Follow the Sun" because she does follow the sun. Searching for the light source of all being was the inspiration for this quilt, she says. With a last name of "Golden," how could she not be a sun worshipper? When her family lived in Tacoma, Washington, she realized how important sunshine was to her. She follows the sun as it shines through the windowpanes from one side of her house to the other, just as the sun follows its path across the heavens. To feel the rays of the warm sun on her face is heaven, she proclaims. Add a gentle breeze and no work at all will get done that day, she laughs. Her inspiration for this quilt was only the title of the song. The background fabric, hand-dyed by Melody Johnson and Laura Wasilowski, reminded her of the colorful '60s era. The spiraling sun is reminiscent of the pop icons of the time. The drone-like images of those following the sun's

Commercial and purchased hand-dyed fabric; fusible appliquéd, machine-quilted.

rays refer to the culture of the '50s, which was the antithesis of the '60s pop culture. Large raindrops fill in the background quilting design.

Quilting has provided Paula with a connection to quilters of other eras. As her military family relocated many times throughout her life, she has never felt rooted in any location. Quilting gives her the feeling of being in a continuum of women and men who have shared this interest over hundreds of years. It also provides her with almost instant friendships as she visits quilt shows and conferences. This common bond has brought her into contact with many lovely people she otherwise would not have met. Quilting has also given her learning and growing experiences. The connectedness between human beings provided through quilts and the quilting process improves the quality of life to all those touched by it, she explains.

Paula was a medical technologist with specialty certification in blood banking. She loved that work; in addition to cross-matching, antibody identification provided mini-mysteries to be solved. Now she teaches quilt-making internationally. She also loves to garden and watch the birds.

Rosemary Hinterreger Kelley • West Springfield, Virginia

Calling herself a moderate Beatles fan, Rosemary liked their original albums, but really didn't care for their later work. She wasn't born until after the British invasion had already occurred, but at the age of eight, she was given a portable record player for Christmas. Her parents included the *Introducing the Beatles* album, which she alternated listening to with her *Partridge Family* album.

Although Rosemary likes the Beatles and grew up hearing their songs, they were long broken up when she started really paying attention to the radio. However, she has always loved the Beastie Boys. They broke race and religion barriers by becoming the first Jewish Caucasian rappers to make it on the national airwaves. They are of her era and, like the Beatles, they brought a unique sound to the music world. Most people don't juxtapose these groups, but there are some similarities in terms of their early history. When they first traveled to the U.S., the Beatles were considered scandalous by the American press. When the Beastie Boys did their first London tour, they were vilified by the British press for their crazy concerts and new sound, as well. The Beatles really changed rock and roll post-1964. The Beastie Boys completely changed the image of rap as a purely urban genre and brought it to a broader audience.

When Rosemary first entered high school, rap did not have a big following in her upper middle-class

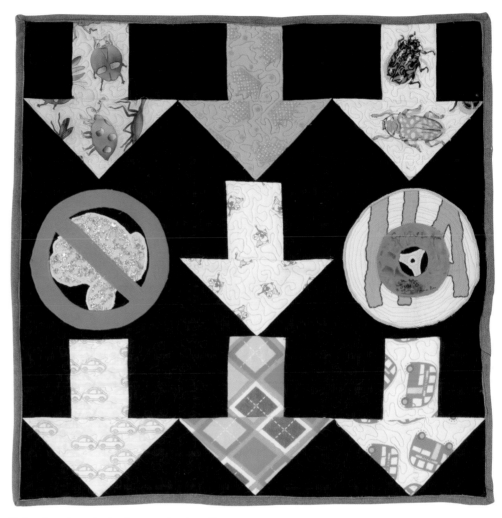

Cotton, flannel, sequins, beads; paper-pieced, machine-appliquéd, embellished.

suburban high school, and she endured six painful years of violin and orchestra and three years playing the bells for marching band. However, her biology lab partner happened to be from inner city Boston and he introduced her to the rhythm and rhymes of old school rap. She was one of the few suburban kids who liked rap in her day, she contends proudly.

Rosemary took needlepoint classes in the fifth grade. In junior high, she spent a third of a year each in sewing, graphic arts, and fine art. She sewed all of the owl mascot pillows for Kappa Kappa Gamma, her sorority at Carnegie Mellon. She made a very traditional, mauve and dusty blue quilt in 1989, as these were the typical colors of that time period, and she vowed to never do that again. In 1995, thanks to Margaret Rolfe's book *Quilt a Koala*, she discovered exciting designs and colors and resumed quilting, which she finds relaxing. In her younger days as a stay-at-home mom and an officer's wife, she enjoyed taking on projects with permanent results. Meals get eaten, laundry and houses get dirty again, and the lawn keeps growing. Doing something that did not come undone made her so happy, she says.

When she heard about this quilt challenge, Rosemary recalls, "I knew 'I'm Down' would be the perfect song to depict," as there were versions sung by both the Beatles and the Beastie Boys. Rosemary designs picture quilts and chooses her fabric accordingly; however, in this particular quilt, she acknowledges she is "rebelling, as usual," by making it about the Beatles and the Beastie Boys singing this song. Because of that, she felt the obvious need for directional arrows. The seven arrows represent the four Beatles and three Beastie Boys; the four Beatles' arrows either have beetle insects, beetle cars, or London double decker buses as motifs.

The only music that has truly had an effect on her was by the Beastie Boys, says Rosemary. Those musicians are her age, so their sophomoric lyrics amused her when she was young and, as they aged and evolved, so did she. She credits them for getting her through cancer treatment and the devastation it had on her family. Rosemary is a campus dean for Webster University.

"I'M HAPPY JUST TO DANCE WITH YOU"

Donna Marcinkowski DeSoto • Fairfax, Virginia

Batiks, commercial cotton, silk, ultra-suede, various fibers, beads, freshwater pearls, seashells; raw edge appliquéd, machine-pieced and quilted, hand-stitched and embellished.

The year 1964 was a remarkable year for Donna's family. They were living in Fort Richardson, Alaska, where her dad was an army officer. On Good Friday of that year, the Great Alaskan Earthquake occurred, with a magnitude of a whopping 9.2. Before that earthquake, though, came something just as earth-shaking: the Beatles appeared on *The Ed Sullivan Show*. She was just seven years old, Donna recalls, but "as I watched my mom react, smiling and moving to the music in a way I had never seen her move before, I knew this was big."

Years later, as Donna and Kurt prepared for their wedding, she thought it was important for them to take dance lessons. "I wanted to look smooth and natural as we danced to music by a live band at our reception," she explains. They signed up for a crash course on social dance, tripping, dipping, and slipping through the waltz, the tango,

the cha-cha, and the hustle, among others. Their moves never did end up "looking smooth or feeling natural," as they muddled their way through on the big day. Luckily, no videos exist to prove this true.

A few days later, on their honeymoon in the Virgin Islands, the two of them stood under a warm, balmy sky bursting with shooting stars. It was just after midnight and reggae music played far in the distance. They were barefoot, swaying in each other's arms, accompanied by the rustle of trade winds in a mango tree and in the oleander. This is the story Donna's quilt tells. "I'm Happy Just to Dance with You" is not only one of her favorite Beatles tunes, but Donna muses, "I have come to learn that what matters most is just the dancing, plain and simple. When you have someone at your side, missteps aren't important. It's all about the being there, that way of dancing in unplanned, unrehearsed steps that make up a lifetime together."

"I'M LOOKING THROUGH YOU"

Susan Egge Haftel • Gainesville, Virginia

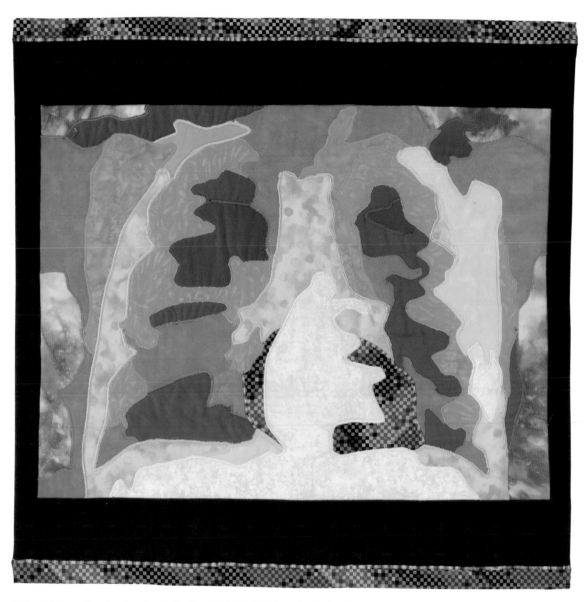

Cotton fabric; appliquéd as described in Replique Quilts by Chris Lynn Kirsch. The base image is from a public domain clip art image of an x-ray found on clker.com.

Susan was just fourteen years old when the British invasion started. Of all the groups involved in the musical takeover of the United States, the Beatles were her favorites.

When she was three years old, Susan started sewing buttons to scraps of fabric. She took up quilting in the mid-1970s and, because she had made practically every traditional pattern known by the year 2000, she looked for something new to challenge herself with. It's not the act of sewing three layers of fabric and quilting that she loves — it's the challenge "of designing and adapting the techniques that will bring them to life," she enthuses.

Susan's art quilt teacher often encourages her students to get out of their comfort zone and the idea of the Beatles art quilt challenge

was, initially, quite uncomfortable, Susan acknowledges. Now, though, she's convinced she needs to participate in more challenges. Her inspiriation for "I'm Looking Through You" was Paul's relationship with Jane Asher. Her quilt is a pun about "looking through" someone. While making the quilt, she had a dozen different ideas and was experimenting with one when she suddenly ditched it and began this quilt. She didn't stop working on the new design until it was finished. This seems to be typical of her design process. "My muse never visits until she can pull the rug out from under me," Susan reveals.

Susan taught middle school English, on and off, for thirty years. If she didn't already sew, then she would learn to. "There is nothing else," she divulges.

"I'M ONLY SLEEPING"

Andrea Blackmon • Alexandria, Virginia

Andrea's father was stationed in Germany when she was young. Every Saturday they went to the movies because a different one played each week. When she was seven or eight, one of the Beatles movies was playing. She had never heard of them before and thought they weren't a real group. She thought the screaming women were fake and they gave her a really good laugh. She liked the music, though. By the time she saw the second movie, "I learned they were a real group and that women really did act like that," she laughs.

Andrea works in Human Services in a vocational program with adults who have developmental disabilities. She has seen first-hand how music helps some of them concentrate. One of the participants even requests the Beatles music to listen to. When they play a Beatles compilation CD, "It makes everyone happy...They dance a bit and then everyone gets back to work," she states.

As a teenager, Andrea sang in the church youth choir. In junior high, she sang second soprano in the girl's Glee Club. She listens to all kinds of music: jazz, rhythm and blues, rock, country, world music, and classical. Music uplifts her spirits. Even if she is sad and listens to sad music, it makes her feel better. As for the effect it has on her creative process, "I am most productive when I'm listening to music or a book on tape," she reveals.

When she was ten years old, Andrea asked her mother to teach her to sew. She began making her own clothes in the fifth grade and has been sewing for more than forty years now. One day, she visited her childhood Girl Scout leader who was living in an assisted living apartment, and the woman told Andrea she wanted a quilt. When Andrea said that she didn't know how to make one, the woman responded, "You know how to sew, you know how to quilt." Andrea took a quilting class, but, unfortunately, the woman died before her quilt was completed.

Andrea has been involved in an art quilt group for four years. She has only made two other art quilts besides this one, although she has many assignments that could be turned into art quilts. She was having a difficult time selecting a song when a co-worker, who also likes the Beatles, looked at the list and encouraged her to choose "I'm Only Sleeping." Andrea wasn't familiar with the song, so she found it online and listened to it several times. The lyrics inspired this quilt; they describe the sleepiness felt just before waking.

Andrea used a photo she took of a sunrise at the Outer Banks to represent the time of day. She took a photo of her nephew in bed, shrank it, and cut and fused it to another photo of a river to represent lying in bed and floating upstream. Both of those photographs became

Cotton fabric, cotton and wool-blend yarn, fusible vinyl; appliquéd, computer-printed on fabric, photo collaged.

the pictures above the bed. In the window is a collage of photos she has taken of friends and family going places or doing things. Her sister gave her a disc that came with Photoshop® Elements 8, and that's what she used to make the collage and the two pictures above the bed. A lot of time and ink was used in the process!

Nancy Karst • Springfield, Virginia

Cotton fabric dyed by Marie Wiley, personal photos printed on fabric, vintage buttons, beads, and personal trinkets collected from family and friends for more than fifty years; hand- and machine-quilted, embroidered.

Nancy has been a Beatles fan since "Love Me Do." She remembers the night when they appeared on *The Ed Sullivan Show*. Though she was not one to swoon, scream, or faint over them, she has loved them and their music for most of her life. Recently, she downloaded a lullaby rendition of the Beatles' songs with the hope her newborn granddaughter will also become a fan. So far, her granddaughter seems intrigued. "Maybe it is the bells and the mellotron, but the baby loves to listen and 'In My Life' is one of the selections. She seems to find the music soothing, just as I do," Nancy explains.

Nancy listens to a lot of different types of music and even audio books while she sews. For her, there is nothing like a sad song to inspire art, and she discloses that "In My Life" brings back a lot of memories. She played the song over and over after her cousin was killed in the Vietnam War. All these years later, she thinks of him whenever she hears this song.

It also makes her think of her teenage years, how far she has come, and all the people she has met along the way.

Nancy quilted names of people and places on the quilt. As she stitched, she thought about family, school friends, and the places she has been. In script, she did free motion quilting of the names in a circle. The design is a mandala. She chose trees of the four seasons as the gates, or corners, of the design.

One of the memories Nancy has from her childhood is of her grandmother teaching her to embroider when she was about eight years old. Her grandmother was a skilled needlewoman and Nancy loved to visit her in the old Victorian house with settees and plates on the walls. She was only eleven when her grandmother passed away, but "I'll never lose affection." Now, Nancy hopes to pass those needle skills onto her granddaughter.

Doris Judge • Gainesville, Virginia

Cotton fabric, quilters' taffeta, embroidery threads, and printable fabric; raw edge appliquéd, embroidered and free motion quilted. Embroidery is based on Fanciful Stitches, Colorful Quilts by Laura Wasilowski. Donna Meyer painted the top of the mountains, and Ane Haycraft advised on perspective. The helicopter image was downloaded from the Internet with permission from James Harrington.

After seeing the Beatles on *The Ed Sullivan Show*, Doris was hooked. She listens to all kinds of music, depending on her mood, because she finds it uplifting.

Doris has been sewing since she was a child, raised in Germany. She enjoys quilting because it is a way to create something beautiful, as well as useful. Plus, she remarks, "Sharing this hobby with friends has enriched my social life."

Doris decided to use the song "It Won't Be Long" because there is something comforting about anticipating a homecoming, be it from war, vacation, or travel. She joined the Beatles Art Quilt Challenge because she wanted to "challenge" herself. She confesses that her quilt was inspired by telecasts of troops returning home from war. Doris reveals further, "It did turn out to be a hard challenge, especially since this is my first original art quilt, but I am glad I tried something new."

Doris' favorite quilting style is needle turn appliqué. She also loves hand-quilting. She has volunteered for the last two years teaching quilting to some lovely ladies at the Senior Center in Manassas, Virginia. Any handwork makes her happy — sewing, knitting, and crocheting — and she is very proud to have had the quilt, *Chesapeake Rose*, published in the magazine *Quilting Today*. She later gave that quilt to her daughter and son-in-law. If she didn't stitch, Doris says, "I would probably do more volunteer work." Next, she plans to make a quilt for her daughter's new house.

"JOHNNY B. GOODE"

Lori East • Carthage, Missouri

Cotton fabric; paper-pieced, raw edge appliquéd, thread sketched.

The Beatles' music has been around her entire life, Lori muses, "so in a way, it is the background for my life story." Today, music has a huge impact on her creative process; it is almost always playing in her workroom. Different moods and various pieces "need different sorts of sounds," she explains.

Lori has been sewing nearly all of her life. She got a sewing machine and made her first quilt when she was nine. Lori considers all quilts art. "Each is a representation of the way the quilt maker sees things," she offers. She realized she "saw things differently" when she worked in a quilt shop and saw how many people wanted to make a quilt exactly like the samples hanging in the shop. She remembers thinking, "why would they want to make something that was indistinguishable from someone else's quilt?"

Lori is continually fascinated with the way each of us sees things. Ten different people will interpret one thing in ten different ways, which, she feels, makes life interesting. She participates in challenges because they provide opportunities for her to try things she might not otherwise do and to share a vision with others. She works with all sorts of material,

from vintage blocks to plastic bags. She loves the steady rhythm of a traditional quilt as much as the fabulous graphic treat of a studio quilt.

Lori chose "Johnny B. Goode" because she always loved the song. "It's interesting to translate what is in your head to fabric," she says, explaining that she was "sometimes frustrated and other times crazy excited" about the way things came together. In the end, it was a huge learning experience, she adds. Lori put her life on hold to make this quilt since she only learned about the challenge slightly more than two weeks before the deadline. She took three days off to can beets, but other than that, not much else got done. Her husband even cooked supper for a couple of nights to help out.

Lori's to-do list is always long. She has several quilts in progress, a huge research project she hopes to publish soon, and maybe another challenge or two. She is a certified appraiser of quilts and quilted textiles, a past board member of the American Quilt Study Group, "and an all-around quilt addict." In her day-to-day life, she is a wife, home-schooling mom to "the smartest boy on the planet," and an unabashed Christian.

"KANSAS CITY/HEY-HEY-HEY-HEY!"

Sue Graham • Ashburn, Virginia

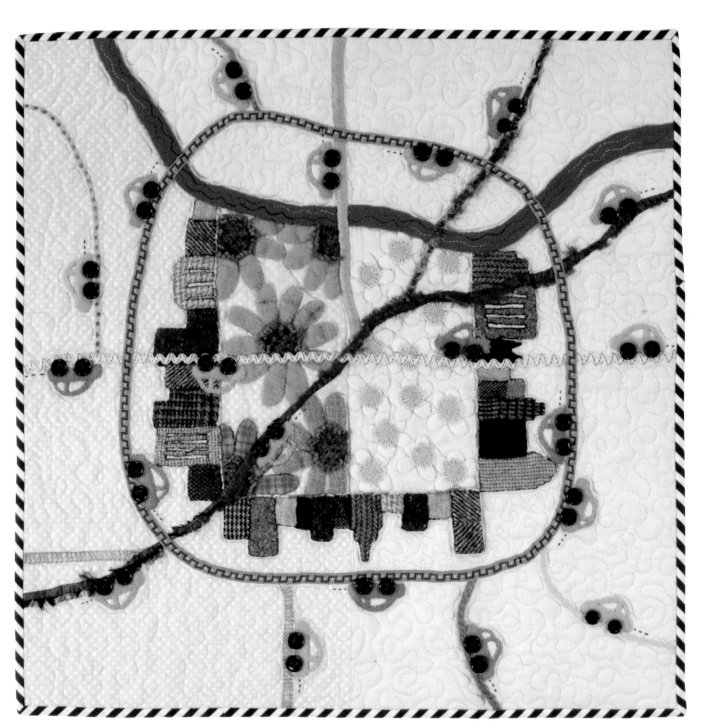

*Cotton fabric, wool, vintage ribbon, sari silk, miscellaneous trims;
hand-embellished, machine-quilted.*

Reverse of quilt by Sue Graham.

Sue is an early Beatles fan, pre-drugs, sitar, and politics, and she is currently a Sir Paul fan. She was glued to *The Ed Sullivan Show* for both nights when they were on in February 1964, and also remembers seeing them on the 1960s variety shows *Shindig!* and *Hullabaloo*. She was in junior high school and begged permission from her mom to buy a fifty-cent Beatles fan magazine. She remembers trying to decide which one to buy and finally chose two twenty-five-cent magazines. She wishes she had kept them.

She doesn't listen to much music, Sue says, because "songs get stuck in my head for too many days and nights," but she loves almost all music: classical, jazz, some modern pop, rhythm and blues, and hip hop. After studying piano and clarinet, she trained in voice and sang many solos in church and school choirs. The funny thing is that all she really wanted to do musically was to be a girl singer, with a tambourine, in a rock and roll band.

Several of Sue's earliest memories are of sewing. Her mother was gifted at sewing all clothing, including coats and prom gowns, as well as draperies, and slipcovers. Her mother also knitted and quilted. Sue remembers choosing buttons from the button box and sewing them onto fabric scraps at the age of four or five. She has four embroidered pieces hanging in her home that she made as a child. In high school, she designed and sewed clothes for herself. She gave up sewing clothes in 1980 and became an ardent quilter.

The moment she heard about the Beatles quilt challenge, Sue says she knew she had to participate. "This is the most fun quilt challenge I have ever been involved in!" she enthuses. She chose "Kansas City/ Hey-Hey-Hey-Hey!" because of the title. She was born in Kansas City, Missouri. Even though this Beatles song isn't recognized by most, it has some solid rhythm and blues history. Her quilt is a happy version of a map of the conjoined Kansas cities, with sunflowers filling downtown Kansas City, Kansas, and hawthorn blossoms filling downtown Kansas City, Missouri. The car design was particularly interesting. In her first sketch, Sue explains, she drew a generic little car. When she found the backing fabric, she modified the window design on her little fleet of cars. Her husband pointed out that the design was that of a Volkswagon Beetle. She hadn't realized it before, but found it amusing: Beatles/Beetle, how fun.

Sue primarily makes traditional quilts, but she loves the creativity and freedom of designing art quilts. She quilts because "I am not happy without a needle in my hand or my foot on the sewing machine pedal." Sometimes she thinks about the hundreds of quilts she will leave behind and the many people who will have them.

Sue claims that all she ever really wanted to be when she grew up was a wife and mother. She used to love homemaking, but now feels it is work and takes too much time away from her quilting. She is proud to have had a quilt accepted into the Pennsylvania National Quilt Extravaganza. She works part-time, but that's mostly to support her quilting habit. The license plate on her car says it all: WANAQLT.

"LADY MADONNA"

Beth Meenehan • Fairfax, Virginia

Cotton fabric, pens, acrylic paint; drawn, painted, and thread painted.

Beth has been a Beatles fan since 1964, when her older sister started listening to their 45s on her turntable. She was brokenhearted when they split up and, later, she was devastated when John was killed. Today, she enjoys listening to musicals, rock and roll, folk, jazz, country, classical, and Christmas music.

Beth notes she has been sewing "forever." Her mother was an avid hand quilter and Beth used to cut pieces to help make wedding ring quilts. There were 1,400 pieces per quilt — and that was *before* the rotary cutter was invented — so the cutting alone took a long time, she recalls.

The song "Lady Madonna" called out to Beth, as her passion is making religious art quilts. Beth wanted to pay tribute to the four men who changed the music world forever by making a Beatles-themed art quilt, and she is inspired by her belief in the intercession of the Blessed Virgin Mary. There have been many times when she has changed her life, Beth discloses.

Quilting keeps her sane in a crazy world, Beth laughs. She makes charity quilts for disaster relief and also collects those that others make and

sends them to those in need. Most recently, quilts were sent to Hurricane Sandy and Moore, Oklahoma, tornado victims. This reminds Beth that a few good women can make a big difference in someone's life by caring enough to make quilts from the heart and giving them to strangers.

Beth works as the night supervisor of a small psychiatric hospital in Falls Church, Virginia. Outside of work she is a member of the Daughters of the American Revolution. "Many think that it's a gathering of old ladies who drink punch and tea and eat the latest prize-winning cake," she observes, "but it is, in fact, a women's service organization that promotes patriotism, education, and respect for history and family values."

The most important thing Beth wants people to know about her is she has been married to Michael, her best friend, for thirty-two years and they have two amazing kids: Marty, 28, and Meggie, 22. She and Michael have been through a lot, but everything that happens brings them closer together. She gets a love letter from him everyday — and she has for over 8,000 days.

"LET IT BE"

Cyndi Zacheis Souder • Annandale, Virginia

As part of a fundraiser in college, Cyndi delivered singing Valentines. A dear friend played the guitar and they sang "All My Loving" wherever they were sent. They worked out harmonies and had a great time, she recalls. Cyndi likes their music, but says she is not a rabid Beatles fan.

Cyndi listens to almost any kind of music. Her musical choices depend on what she is doing. Music fills the empty spaces, keeps her company, energizes her, calms her, helps her sleep, and helps her focus, she says. It also provides her with a soundtrack for her creative endeavors. When she is designing, she usually listens to soft music without lyrics so there is no competition for attention in her brain. When she is creating the quilt top and then quilting, she often has a soundtrack for the piece.

Music has always been a part of Cyndi's life. Growing up, she was expected to play at least one musical instrument. Her first instrument was a ukulele. Later, she played the clarinet and oboe. She dabbled with the Celtic harp and the fife, and played the contrabassoon.

Cyndi has been sewing since she was a child because, she explains, "if you were a girl child in my family, you learned the needle arts." She started quilting in college. Her sister taught her traditional quilting by hand. As Cyndi learned machine-piecing and appliqué techniques, and as commercially available tools and fabrics advanced, she transitioned to machine work and left commercial patterns behind. She gained confidence in art quilt classes with Judy House and in a project Judy organized called "Healing Quilts in Medicine." Currently, "I mostly make art quilts, and I love helping traditional quilters make the jump to art quilts."

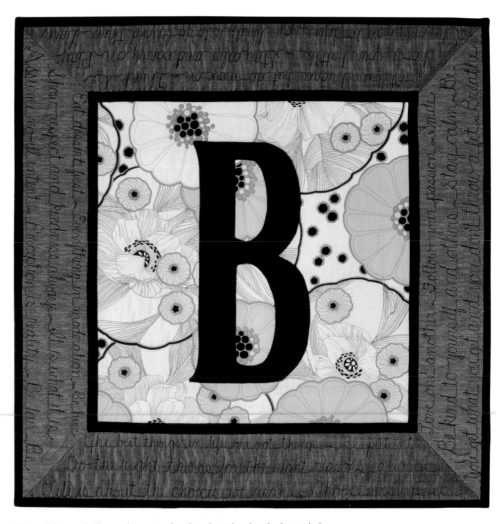

Cotton fabric and silk; machine-pieced and appliquéd and quilted to include quilt writing, Cyndi's own method of free motion quilting.

Cyndi says she enjoys the restrictions of a challenge. While we sometimes chafe beneath the imposition of rules and themes, all quilts have rules. In a challenge, someone sets the guidelines. When she is working with someone else's vision, it forces her to create differently and she grows from the experience, Cyndi explains, adding that she feels the quilting stitches are as important as the piecing or appliqué work. In this case, she used her quilt writing technique to include words of wisdom in keeping with the intention of the lyrics. This quilt came to be as a result of her love of fonts and strong, simple designs.

Sewing and quilting give her peace and a sense of satisfaction, Cyndi claims. She loves the planning, the fabric choices, the construction, the joy of the well-sewn seam, and the finished quilt. "From start to finish, the process chases away any troubles or worries I may have. When I'm quilting, all is right with the world," she discloses.

Lynn Droege • Overland Park, Kansas

Cotton fabric, ribbon, crystals, leather, rayon, yarns; paper-pieced and machine-appliquéd, fiber bonded and crystal bonded.

Lynn is "absolutely a Beatles fan" who remembers watching them on *The Ed Sullivan Show* and having her hair cut like Paul's. She finds music to be calming; it helps her to relax and keeps her grounded. She mostly likes rock, country, and Motown. She plays the guitar, which she used to play at Mass on Sundays and at retirement homes.

Lynn learned to sew in 4-H when she was ten years old. Her quilt-making began in 2000, when her son went to college; she only began making art quilts in the last two years. When she thought of "Long Tall Sally," Lynn says, an image popped into her mind. It is one of those songs that the Beatles wrote and other artists made famous. She hadn't realized that the Beatles wrote so many songs and she enjoyed listening to this one, also as sung by Little Richard and Elvis. It depicts a very tall lady walking into a party and knocking everyone's socks off,

and she pictured "a tall gorgeous lady with tons of sass and attitude, looking like she was ready to have fun," Lynn explains.

She also had to think "way outside of the box" in making this quilt because it wasn't done in her typical style, Lynn notes. One thing she really enjoyed about participating in this challenge was the enthusiasm surrounding the project via the Internet by other participants.

Lynn has been employed as a dental hygienist for forty years. She enjoys her life, which includes a son and two grandsons. She has had quilts published, won a national challenge sponsored by Moda Fabrics, and one of her quilts was used on a mug that sold in the National Quilt Museum's gift shop in Paducah, Kentucky. She has served as president for a local quilt guild and is excited to be co-chair of a regional quilt show in 2015 in Kansas City.

Cotton fabric, fusible web, various threads; machine-pieced and quilted, thread painted.

Bonnie is a Beatles fan who, as a freshman at Bridgewater College, gathered with others in the dormitory lounge to watch *The Ed Sullivan Show* and the highly anticipated first performance of the Beatles. It did not disappoint. It was the first time the students had seen the Beatles and they didn't know what to expect. It was quite exciting! "There was just one TV and most sat on the floor, shoulder-to-shoulder," she recalls. Today, Bonnie's kids, who are forty-something, are Beatles fans.

Bonnie played the piano and organ. She also participated in and directed a hand bell choir that played at her wedding. She loves the oldies. She also enjoys show tunes and has memorized the songs in *Les Misérables*, but she mostly listens to classical music throughout the day. Her husband refers to classical music as a "benign narcotic,"

she says, as it has a calming, relaxing effect on her. She also finds it freeing, allowing her to think more creatively.

Bonnie learned about sewing in a high school home economics class. She eventually sewed nearly all of her clothes and later made clothing for her two kids. Her first attempt at appliqué was on a handmade school bag for her son when he started kindergarten. He loved that large green bag with his big initials on it, but just a year later, in the first grade, "it wasn't cool anymore, so it stayed in the closet," she laughs.

Bonnie began quilting in the late 1990s, when a friend invited her to join a quilt group. She loves learning about quilts and quilting, new techniques, and tools. Just in the past several years, she has been "adventurous" in discovering art quilting. She took several classes and workshops and now is drawn to the "out of the box" way of approaching

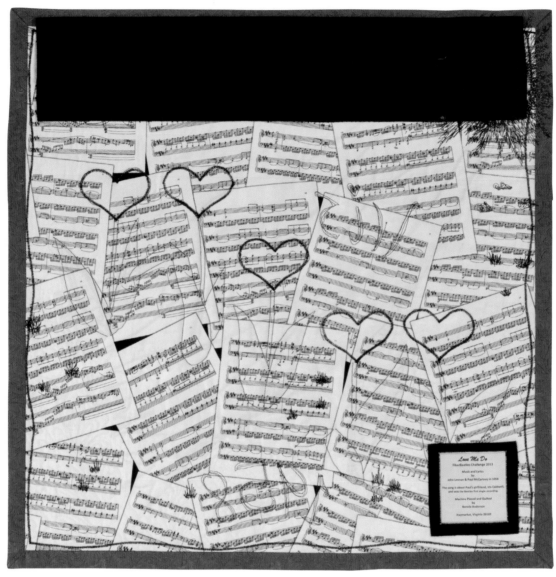

Reverse of quilt by Bonnie Anderson.

an art quilt. She quilts because she loves the feel of fabrics, the colors, the designs, and the process. Her husband, though, is puzzled and doesn't understand "why I cut up perfectly good fabric and then put it back together again," she laughs.

Bonnie adds that she is one of those frustrated crafters who is into everything and, thus, doesn't have enough time for anything. When she retired from an administrative faculty position at George Mason University, she got into pottery, baskets, stained glass, and broken china mosaics. She was lucky enough to be able to sell some of the items she made at craft shows for several years, but then she and her husband down-sized and moved. She couldn't move all of her craft supplies, so now she limits herself to quilting, which, she finds, "has been liberating."

"Love Me Do" is a song written by John and Paul in 1958 when John was seventeen and Paul was sixteen. They made time for song-writing by skipping school. They had written songs before, but this was the first one they liked enough to record as their first single. Paul wrote about his girlfriend at the time, Iris. These three bits of information are incorporated in the quilt design. While making her quilt, Bonnie almost completed it using decorator fabrics from sample books she found at a yard sale. Unfortunately, the thickness of the fabrics wouldn't cooperate with her design, so she started all over again with quilting cottons. Right before the quilt was due, Bonnie was pleasantly surprised to discover all seven members of her quilting bee were participating in this challenge. They had lost track of each other and hadn't met for nearly a year. This got them back together for several outings and get-togethers.

"LOVELY RITA METER MAID"

Shoshana Spiegel • Herndon, Virginia

Cotton fabric, buttons, ribbon; fusible raw edge appliquéd, machine-quilted.

Music is very important to Shana, who studied violin between the ages of ten and fifteen. Though she doesn't play much anymore, she still has the violin and plays it occasionally. Ten years ago, Shana joined Mosaic Harmony, a multi-faith gospel choir, and found singing with a group to be healing. Listening to Jewish spiritual and new age music soothes her. Some nights she uses music to help her get to sleep. She also uses special, electronically-modified music as part of her work with children who have Sensory Processing Disorder.

Shana discovered quilting in the late '70s and did everything by hand at first. She began to use a sewing machine for quilted clothing classes with Lesly-Claire Greenberg. From there, she gradually started machine-piecing and then dabbled in machine-quilting, but she still likes doing handwork because "I find it more relaxing." A few years ago, she took a class from artist Didi Salvatierra, which opened up the possibilities of using color in new ways. It also pushed her to take risks, she says.

Shana chose the song "Lovely Rita" because of the lyrics. She is evolving all the time and enjoys the freedom to explore in her quilting, adding that with this piece she "stretched herself a little" by doing a cartoony style, especially in making the car. She found having a fun project with a deadline "to be therapeutic."

In 2011, Shana created a piece for Sacred Threads called "Facing the Past, Healing the Future" that was both her first original art quilt and a very personal sharing of family Holocaust history. It was published in a journal for Holocaust educators called *PRISM*.

Shana quilts because she enjoys creating and loves fabric. Textures have great appeal to her. Quilting is something in her life "that I have control over, at least most of the time." She is an occupational therapist and Healing Touch practitioner who originally got into the field because she values the use of purposeful activity.

"LUCY IN THE SKY WITH DIAMONDS"

Judith Newman • Fairfax, Virginia

Hand-painted, hand-dyed, and rusted fabric; fusible machine-appliquéd. Machine quilted by Kyoko Yamamura. Special thanks to Susan Bagshaw, who drew the figures and the boat.

Judith grew up during the Elvis rage. She was too busy raising babies during the Beatles era to have any favorites of the Fab Four, although she was very partial to Peter, Paul, and Mary, and Simon and Garfunkle. She loves to work on her art to great music and listens to classical, folk, rock, and Broadway tunes.

Judith has been sewing for sixty-five years. Her quilting passion began twenty-five years ago. This love grew the first time she discovered she didn't have to do everything by hand. She has been playing with ideas for art quilts for as long as she has been quilting. She loves the designing, the color, the putting together, the learning … "Really, the whole process of quilting," she says.

Judith chose "Lucy in the Sky with Diamonds" because it is one of the few Beatles songs she knows well. The song put an immediate picture in her head. The Zentangle® portion of her quilt was based on the technique of meditative drawing developed by Rick Roberts and Maria Thomas. Judith tries many techniques in her artwork and she is always eager to experiment with new things. She takes classes at every opportunity and enjoys making quilts for her family and friends.

Judith was a stay-at-home mom until all of her children were grown and then a mental health counselor and, finally, a soccer referee assignor. Now, besides quilting, Judith raises her granddaughter, reads, and writes. While working on this quilt, she wrote her first book. However, she also put several projects on hold, including making charity quilts for neonatal babies and Oklahoma tornado victims, and looks forward to "resuming work on about five hundred unfinished projects!"

Mary Ellen Simmons • Fairfax, Virginia

Mary Ellen was young and newly married, living in New Orleans in the mid-1960s, when the Beatles were reaching great popularity. She remembers that time well: beautiful New Orleans, the Vietnam War, and the Beatles.

Mary Ellen frequently takes long road trips and finds that music always makes the trip seem shorter. Most of her studio time, however, is spent listening to books on tape, but when she really needs to concentrate to figure something out, she works in silence.

During the summer of 1990, Mary Ellen wanted to try something different, so she took a week-long class with artist Nancy Crow. It was her first foray into art quilting. Now, she is committed to all forms of quilting — "I love the process, the journey, and the end product," Mary Ellen divulges. She has also met wonderful people and cherishes being a part of the quilting community. She quilts for the creativity, "but also for the companionship and friendships."

Mary Ellen chose "Magical Mystery Tour" because it is the title song on her favorite Beatles album, which her brother gave her for her twenty-fifth birthday. She was living in Staten Island as a new mother and was alone with her baby all day as her husband went to Manhattan for work. She played the album a lot, dancing around with her son, John, in her arms and singing that they were going to go on a "magical mystery tour." In planning this quilt, she thought of a wizard casting a magical spell and calling everyone to go on a world tour with her to the sites of some of the unsolved mysteries of the world. She hand-painted the background to resemble oceans. She drew the outline of the countries of the world and hand-appliquéd, fused, and stitched the wizard and the people to the background.

Mary Ellen feels privileged to live in the Washington, D.C., area and to have had many wonderful teachers and mentors. She has enjoyed abundant opportunities to take lectures, classes, and workshops; her "Magical Mystery Tour" quilt contains skills practiced in many different classes. She is a busy member of Quilters Unlimited, the Sister's Choice Quilters in Falls Church, Virginia, and the Blue Ridge Quilters of Johnson City, Tennessee. One of her quilts is pictured in Jinny Beyer's *Medallion Quilts* book and she is featured in *Dare to Dance, An Art Quilt Challenge*. In addition, an early art quilt was pictured in *Ladies Circle Patchwork* while another quilt recently appeared in *Quilt Trends*. She also felt honored to have her work in the Sacred Threads exhibitions.

Hand-painted and commercial cotton fabric, sequins and beads, buttons, metallic ribbon, rayon tassels, various types of thread and fabric pens, metallic fabric paint; drawing, painted, machine-appliquéd and quilted, hand-embellished.

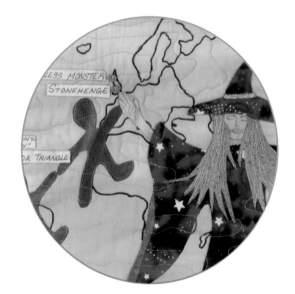

"MAXWELL'S SILVER HAMMER"

Jason Wolfson • Chantilly, Virginia

Cotton fabric; fusible appliquéd, paper-pieced, machine-stitched.

Jason likes the Beatles, but doesn't consider himself an obsessive fan. He was a young child in the mid-seventies and his babysitters used to listen to the Beatles all the time. He prefers groups like Pink Floyd, Led Zeppelin, David Bowie, and Emerson, Lake and Palmer.

This is Jason's first quilt. He did it to see if he could actually make one since his wife, Karen, makes quilts all the time. "Karen can do all sorts of wonderful things with fabric," he marvels. He adds that the Beatles Art Quilt Challenge "seemed interesting enough to give (quilting) a try."

Jason chose "Maxwell's Silver Hammer" because he thought "if I could make something artful from a rather catchy song about a serial killer who beat people with a hammer, then why not?" Most of the people he spoke to about the song love it, but they never really paid attention to the lyrics. When he tells them what the song is about, they find it hard to believe this catchy tune has such a dark theme.

The first row of three in this quilt is the first verse of the song. The first block represents Joan studying in her room. The second block is Maxwell Edison, who is majoring in medicine. The third block is what Maxwell does to her when he picks her up for the date; he kills Joan. The second row is the second verse. The first block represents Maxwell playing the fool, back in school. (Jason figures throwing paper airplanes is foolish.) In the second block, the teacher has Maxwell stay behind and write fifty times on the blackboard. (This is a coincidence with the Beatles fiftieth anniversary.) In the third block, the teacher turns her back and Maxwell does his thing; he kills the teacher. The third row depicts the third verse. In the first block, P.C. 31 catches Maxwell. In the second, Rose and Valerie are screaming in the gallery, saying he must go free. A bit of artistic liberty was taken here. The third block is the final chorus of Maxwell doing his thing a third time; he kills the Judge.

Jason is a research and development engineer. He enjoys building with Lego®, reading science fiction, and playing video games.

"MEAN MR. MUSTARD"

Sharon McDonagh • Alexandria, Virginia

Cotton, wool, and upholstery fabric, wool roving, cheesecloth, handmade paper, vintage photographs, paper and other ephemera, various trims and embellishments; collaged, mixed media assemblage, machine-quilted, felted, and hand-stitched.

Sharon believes if you enjoy any genre of music, you have to love the Beatles at least a little "They produced such a variety of songs and were so influential," she reasons. Today, she has an abiding affection for '80s music and calls her preference adult alternative. Sharon finds song lyrics to be evocative and thought-provoking. "Many ideas in the creative process can come from music," Sharon explains.

Sharon was a member of 4-H as a child and received sewing lessons through that organization, winning ribbons at the county fair for simple garments. She still basks in the praise she received for matching a wool plaid at the seams of a jumper.

Sharon likes doing challenges because they "force me to create." Left to her own devices, she laughs, "I would have never made a yellow quilt about a 'mean old man,'" but she really enjoyed doing so. In this song, "Mr. Mustard" was an anti-social, hoarding miser. Sharon was

raised Catholic and attended Catholic school for eight years. Because of that, she says it only took her "about two milliseconds" to think of the mustard seed parable. She wanted to work it into the quilt. What she hadn't known, and found fascinating, is that it's not just Christian religions with myths and stories attached to the mustard seed.

A friend gave Sharon a huge bag of upholstery fabric and it contained many mustard-colored prints. In researching mustard, Sharon learned the chief coloring agent for the yellow variety is turmeric, so for the first time she experimented with eco-dyeing. Though she appreciates the vast amount of talent and craftsmanship a traditional quilt requires, Sharon says her own creative impulses are fueled by the wide range of materials and possibilities that art quilting allows.

"MEMPHIS, TENNESSEE"

Debra Gabel • Clarksville, Maryland

Organic cotton fabric, fusible fleece, satin cording; Photoshop digital imagery, faux cord binding, raw edge appliquéd, machine-quilted.

Debra is absolutely a Beatles fan. "The first record I ever bought with my allowance and played on my record player was by the Beatles," she confesses. Today, she listens to alternative, country, hip hop, pop, and Christian music. She finds music to be "a mood stabilizer and enhancer," as she admits, "I often listen to music while drawing or quilting because it creates a 'flow' for my work."

Debra began sewing more than thirty-five years ago; she had a sewing job when she was a teenager. As an artist, art quilting has been her media of choice for almost twenty years. She has a B.F.A. in graphic design from the State University of New York. The song "Memphis, Tennessee" fit in well with her current line of patterns, which all have city themes. She learned about Memphis while making this piece and found out Beale Street is where the music happens. She enjoyed listening to the Beatles while making the quilt and is excited this design will eventually be in her "Zebra Patterns" collection.

Debra is a professional quilt pattern designer who has produced more than three hundred raw-edge appliqué patterns. Not only has she authored four books, but she also travels internationally to lecture and instruct on her design process.

Cotton fabric, telephone cord, crystals, buttons; machine-appliquéd and quilted.

Michelle considers herself a Beatles fan "only because my dad liked the song 'Michelle' and named me after it." Her preference, though, is country music.

Michelle has been sewing for about two-and-a-half years. She says she was most likely "bitten by the bug" when she went to her first "Ultimate Fabric Sale" at the Quilt Haus in New Braunfels, Texas. Even though she didn't sew at the time, she purchased fabric, which she still has today. When her sister, Laura, went on a trip for a couple of months to Japan, Michelle was bored, so she started researching quilting online and made three quilt tops by the time Laura returned. Michelle describes herself as a "math person" who likes the piecing aspect of quilting. She is a confessed "fabric hoarder" who particularly enjoys modern fabrics. Her Beatles-themed quilt is her only art quilt.

On this quilt is a representation of a telephone. "Ma Bell" is what the phone company used to be called. Also shown on the quilt are three depictions of "I love you" because of the repetition of that line in the song: one is in sign language, one is in Braille, and one is in French, since some of the words in the song are sung in French. There are also telephone poles and telephone lines to add to the Ma Bell theme. The telephone company puts a number on every telephone pole, and Michelle used the digits on the phone to spell out "Michele," though, she laughs, "it had to have one less 'L' because telephone numbers are only seven digits and not eight." She also, amusingly, wonders if people will be able to interpret the phone number using an old-fashioned telephone.

A high school math teacher, Michelle's next plans are to make baby quilts for two co-workers and a cousin.

Cotton fabric; fusible machine-appliquéd, pieced, and quilted, hand-embellished. Special thanks to Dianne Thomas, who drew the pot at the end of the rainbow.

Nancy is a Beatles fan now, but confesses "I totally ignored them when they first came to America." She took classical violin and piano classes when she was young. Music plays a big role in her life and, in fact, helped bring her together with her second husband. They met on a blind date and listened to big band music at the Rose Haven Yacht Club at Harrington Harbor, Maryland. They used to listen to music together while working in the yard via several sets of outdoor speakers.

Nancy was a fairly traditional quilter until her friend, Beth Meenehan, insisted she attend art quilt meetings beginning in 2007. Nancy admits she has been slow to embrace art quilts because "I love precise, traditional piecing," but contends she is finally enjoying the process and techniques of art quilting.

While on vacation with her daughter, Fonda, Nancy told her about this challenge. She didn't know any Beatles songs except for "When I'm Sixty-Four" — and that song was already claimed. Fonda insisted she knew more songs than she realized and proceeded to sing many of them. She convinced Nancy she should make a quilt for the song "Money." The "FB Bank" on her quilt represents "Fiber Beatles," the original name of the art quilt challenge.

At one time, Nancy was a program manager for the Navy, but she is now an avid traveler. While working on this quilt, she and her friend, Trudi Sommerfield, went on an exciting trip to see the Sisters Quilt Show in Oregon. Nancy says if she didn't sew, "I would do more gardening and reading."

"MOONLIGHT BAY"

Barbara S. Bockman • Fairfax, Virginia

Cotton and synthetic fabrics, fabric paints; free hand drawing, stenciled, hand-appliquéd, and machine-pieced.

Barbara appreciates much of the work the Beatles did. She sang in school choirs, took piano lessons for a long time, and enjoyed going to the opera and attending classical concerts, but she says all of that is behind her now.

Barbara received fine art instruction from American University. She likes the tactile and three-dimensional effects of fabric and enjoys being able to combine her painting skills with sewing. Barbara thinks quilts are "neat"; she has been sewing them since the early 1970s.

For Barbara, "Moonlight Bay" evokes memories of a performance of that old song by the Beatles. In this quilt, she made an amalgam of a framed picture and a miniature traditional quilt: borders and binding surround a central design to produce an interesting pictorial and tactile wall piece. The use of commercially-printed cottons along with stenciled shapes

expanded the tension of abstract versus realism. Scarab beetle shapes give weight to the lower border and the photo negative effect of the design allows for emphasis on the Union Jack red, white, and blue. The sight line flows from the ovals of the scarabs to the circle of the moon, smoothly moving the eye through the composition. Barbara says she participated in the Beatles art quilt challenge for the chance to be expressive. "Something special that occurs when creativity happens is concentration," she muses.

Barbara's busy life has included roles as an executive secretary, a homemaker and mother, and a gallery member and partner. She has done book illustrations and editing, and has given private drawing and painting lessons. Besides stitching, she paints with watercolor and black oil and acrylics. She also makes block prints. If she didn't sew, Barbara says, "I'd do more painting or try gardening design."

"MOTHER NATURE'S SON"

Lisa Ellis • Fairfax, Virginia

Cotton fabric, buttons; raw edge appliquéd, machine-pieced, and quilted.

Lisa is a Beatles fan who well remembers the media frenzy over the rumors regarding Paul's death. She and her older brother looked for all of the clues and played their records backwards to hear the famous phrases. She took piano lessons as a child and then picked up the guitar in high school. She played the guitar for many years at coffee shops and also led church and youth groups in music. Music creates a connection to the sacred and brings her peace, she muses. She admits to needing to have music playing "when I am making art in order to turn off my left brain and allow my right brain the freedom to create. This extra-sensory input helps me to focus on the creative process."

Through an elementary quilting lesson in the mid-1990s by a friend at church, Lisa hand-pieced and quilted a sampler quilt. She got a sewing machine and started quilting in August 2003. She then taught herself machine-piecing, appliqué, and quilting by watching TV programs and reading quilting books. She started making art quilts immediately. She sews because she enjoys the creative process, the tangible expression of herself, and "I value the connection with other like-minded people."

The song "Mother Nature's Son" appealed to her because of its nature theme, Lisa explains. In making this quilt, she used her Lazy Landscape technique of creating abstracts. She worked on it from her vacation home on the West Coast. Lisa's passion is to make the world a better place through a love for quilting and she heads up two organizations: Sacred Threads and Healing Quilts in Medicine. At one time, she was a missile defense radar engineer. She says if she didn't sew "I'd play the piano more and write music."

116

*Silk, cotton, and synthetic fabrics, silver and glass beads;
machine-quilted, hand-appliquéd and beaded.*

Jane remembers first watching the Beatles on *The Ed Sullivan Show* in February 1964 when she was sixteen. Later that year, she saw them perform at the Hollywood Bowl. She made a Beatles scrapbook, which she still has today. This is somewhat surprising as she was in a military family and they moved many times, often leaving treasures behind. She and her girlfriends collected Beatles bubblegum cards. She also has a large poster of the Fab Four, which is framed and hangs on a wall in her home. She saw all of their movies and used to know most of their music by heart.

"Mr. Moonlight" takes Jane back to the days of her youth. Her interest in and love of the Beatles is what prompted her to enter this challenge, her first quilt challenge. The moon is a simple shape, yet the simplicity and complexity of life is wrapped up in it. The moon represents the mystery of life. The four stars on her quilt represent the four Beatles: John, Paul, Ringo, and George. "Mr. Moonlight" was one of the earlier songs they recorded when they dressed alike, so the stars on the quilt are all relatively the same. Jane feels the Beatles made an overwhelming impression that has lasted to this day, across generations and across cultures.

Jane loves working with fabric and enjoys the interaction of color and design. She insists she doesn't really have a particular quilting style, as she enjoys making both art quilts and more traditional quilts.

"NORWEGIAN WOOD"

Diane Yim • Annandale, Virginia

Cotton fabric, fabric pens, fringe, wooden chopsticks, and other embellishments; trapunto, machine-pieced, and appliquéd.

Diane was a young mother with two little kids when the Beatles first hit the music scene and admits she wasn't really a fan back then. Now she is a fan of their melodies, which have become enduring standards: "Yesterday" and "Michelle," for example.

Diane has a decent singing voice, but she is best at humming along with the melodies. Her quilt buddies at retreats notice this, but it can't be helped — she needs music. She listens often when she is sewing, reading, or traveling because she finds it soothing and comforting. She remembers a time in high school when she was at a new general store in her home town in Lakeview, Oregon. She saw rows and rows of fabrics across the room. "I had a real physical desire to get closer; to go over to them, touch them, buy something, and sew," she explains. She quilts now because the beautiful fabric, the inspiration of other quilters, and the quilting shows she has attended "make this passion too hard to resist."

A friend told her about the quilt challenge and encouraged her to consider "Norwegian Wood" for her song. Diane only recently began doing art quilts by participating in guild challenges. With her iPad, she googled "Norwegian Wood." She recognized the tune, but says she had never connected it to the Beatles. She then researched the lyrics, which made little sense to her; she couldn't see how they related to the title, but she thought the melody was nice and there were quite a few "concrete images I could use": a rug, fireplace, 2:00, wine being consumed, she going off to bed laughing without anything happening, and he going to sleep in the bathtub, then waking and thinking about lighting a fire. Later, she read hilarious interpretations of the lyrics and decided to just go with the scene of the house surrounded by birch tree fabric that she happened to have in her stash. She sketched out the picture and selected the fabrics, adding that she had a lot of fun making this quilt.

Nicki Allen • Springfield, Virginia

Batik, hand-dyed fabric, commercial cottons; machine-pieced, appliquéd, and quilted.

Nicki is a Beatles fan who was "too young to remember when they first took the world by storm." She doesn't play an instrument, nor does she sing or dance very well, "but I love how certain songs make you feel." She has various playlists for different activities, from driving and exercising to cleaning and quilting. Music is part of her day-to-day routine; she mostly listens to classic rock and current pop songs.

Nicki has been sewing since middle school. She took home economics and made a pair of shorts. She wore those shorts everywhere, and still remembers feeling "very proud that I was able to create something I could actually wear." She began making art quilts because she was impressed by the art quilts other quilters created. In 2008, she took a week-long class with artist Janet Fogg at the Empty Spools Seminar in California. The class opened her eyes to a whole new quilting world and helped her find her "inner art quilter," Nicki states.

A research analyst with the Federal Government, Nicki confesses that quilting "is as much a part of my life as eating and breathing…it is therapy, entertainment, friendships, joy, and sometimes frustration." She chose "Ob-la-di, Ob-la-da" because of the story the song describes; it is about the beginnings of a family from the time when two people are attracted to each other. This couple lives happily-ever-after by just living their lives, no matter what life might hold. The characters in this song inspired the quilt. The people aren't complete, but they are there. The "barrow" is a wheelbarrow and, in the background, there are trees with hearts in the quilting, to express more of the love story. She sang the song over and over while making the quilt and adds that "procrastination makes for a sleepless weekend."

Linda M. Moore • Annandale, Virginia

Cotton fabric, buttons, beads; machine-appliquéd and quilted, Kanzashi-method flowers constructed, hand-embellished.

Linda is a Beatles fan. She listens to popular and country music because "it makes me smile and I enjoy working to music." She has been sewing since she was six years old. All types of needlework excite her: embroidery, needlepoint, and smocking, just to name a few. She has taught all sorts of stitching and leads workshops for guilds now. She does many clothing alterations for others, especially on formal and wedding attire. For her son Jacob's wedding two years ago, she made her own dress and the bridesmaid dresses for her daughters. Several years ago, she took a class at the Quilt Patch in Fairfax, Virginia, and began making art quilts.

Linda's oldest daughter, Emma, was four years old when she took dance classes. Her studio did a recital every year, and one year it was to the Beatles' songs. The youngest group, which was the one Emma was in, danced to "Octopus's Garden." Linda remembers the teacher in the middle of the little girls as they held on to the edge of a parachute and danced in and out, around the circle, which is why, on her quilt, flowers dance around the octopus. Today, Linda's youngest daughter, Jenny, is the true Beatles fan in the family and "Octopus's Garden" is one of her favorite Beatles songs, she announces.

Linda acknowledges that she works best under pressure — she made this happy quilt in two weeks, "smiling and humming" most of the time she worked on it. She especially enjoyed making the three-dimensional flowers that are sprinkled and stitched over the surface.

"OLD BROWN SHOE"

Martha Sterrett Schoonmaker • Centreville, Virginia

Cotton, rayon, and faux suede fabric, lace, metal buttons, ribbon; hand-appliquéd and embroidered, machine-pieced and quilted.

Marcie was in her late teens and early twenties when the Beatles were popular. She enjoyed their music, but says she was not a person to become a fan of any particular music group.

Music has always been a major part of Marcie's life, from early elementary school participation to eleven years of piano lessons and singing in high school choirs and at church. Even now she is actively involved in the music program of her church, where she sings and plays English hand bells.

Marcie began sewing as a child when she joined the local 4-H program. She made her first quilt about fifteen years ago, but didn't really become a quilter until five years ago. A member of her church invited other members to join in making quilts for the wounded soldiers at Walter Reed Hospital and taught them the step-by-step process of making a quilt — and Marcie was hooked. She likes belonging to a social group of fun, inspiring women and enjoys "giving my quilts to others as gifts," she states.

When she first started looking over the list of songs, Marcie decided she would pick the first title that she read in which a picture popped into her mind. She had not heard "Old Brown Shoe" before and first pictured a man's old, beat-up shoe. The Victorian theme and shoe idea came to her much later. As she worked with a design of an old, worn-out shoe, she had trouble creating a background to go along with it. She spotted her collection of old lace and the idea of using a Victorian lady's shoe came to mind. She loves old lace and vintage items, particularly the delicacy of tatting, and she has always wanted to create her own crazy quilt. In the end, she designed a quilt so she could work with what she loves and what she is comfortable working with. "A brown Victorian lady's shoe is an old brown shoe, isn't it?" she notes.

Marcie says she loves a good challenge, "especially one that pushes me creatively," and cannot imagine her life without sewing.

"ONLY A NORTHERN SONG"

Kim Gibson • Burke, Virginia

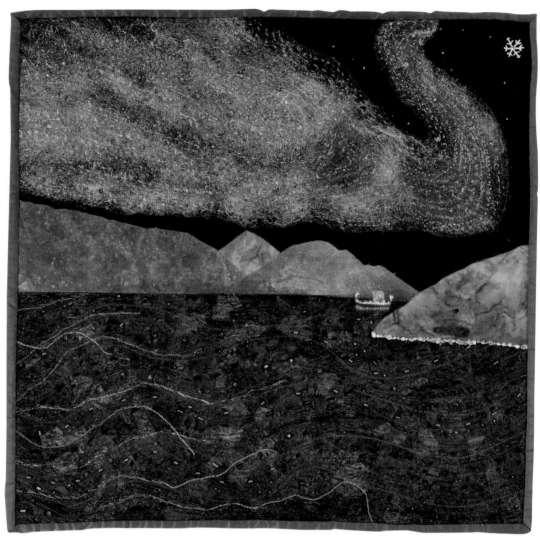

*Wool, Angelina, tulle, polyester, nylon organza, metallic and other embroidery
threads, beads, crystals, paper, puff paint, glitter, and sequins; photo transferred,
hand- and machine-stitched, embellished, beaded.*

Kim liked the Beatles' music when it first came out, but less so when it became more political. She has no musical background or experience, but knows music evokes memories in her. "It can take me back in time and to anywhere in the world," she notes.

Around 1991, Kim began sewing garments with her handwoven fabric and fell in love with surface design. She began dyeing and painting fabrics, and moved on to altering surfaces more dramatically ten years later. After years of pursuing the process, she needed to find a way to apply those techniques to other projects; finally, she began art quilting.

Kim selected "Only A Northern Song" because the title gave her a flash of the aurora borealis. She had numerous instances of personal sightings of this phenomenon and also enjoys seeing photographs of the Northern Lights. She read about the song and its writer, George; the relationship between George and the others was pivotal to the song. She listened to the song a few times and particularly loved the opportunity to

meld the modern music of seminal rock and roll with the ancient Viking burial practice of sending the dead out on the water in a burning ship and the beauty of God's glorious fireworks. The beading and embroidery alone took approximately forty-five hours to complete, she says.

Kim has a special place in her heart for the Quilts of Valor program, and she gives blankets she makes to her local animal shelter. She is also into weaving, spinning, costuming, cooking, reading, living history, bookbinding, and building miniatures. "I have pretty eclectic tastes," she laughs.

Kim spent ten years as a naval officer. She took time off to raise her two children and then entered the retail field. She has taught many subjects, ranging from riding horses, to naval subjects, to science and art. She does extensive historical reenactment and belongs to the Society for Creative Anachronism. "My passion is learning about the old ways, the really old ways — say, one thousand or more years old!" she exclaims.

"PAPERBACK WRITER"

Trudi Sommerfield • Alexandria, Virginia

Commercial and hand-dyed cotton fabric, rubber stamps, hot-fix crystals, gel marker; fusible appliquéd, machine-quilted, and handwritten.

Trudi lived in London for a short time in the 1960s. She was a few years out of college and didn't have a lot of money for clothes, but she liked nice things. She decided to learn to make her own work clothes and save the money she had available in her clothing budget to purchase outfits for dressing up. However, a few days after buying her first sewing machine, she broke her arm while she was ice skating. With her arm in a cast, she couldn't learn to sew. During the time she had a broken arm, she met the man she married. They had a whirlwind romance and, by the time her arm was out of the cast, she was engaged and busy making wedding plans. She didn't learn to use her sewing machine for several months, until after she was married and had moved to Michigan.

Trudi has found quilting to be a fun activity that she enjoys. "Not only does it give me a creative outlet, but it has enabled me to meet the nicest people," she shares. One of the best things about quilting, she adds, is being able to make gifts for new babies, retirees, and wedding couples. She loves fabric and color. "It's so delightful to be able to put together the different colors, patterns, and textures," though she isn't sure what she makes are art quilts. Instead, she calls them "non-traditional wall quilts."

There was so much energy and enthusiasm around this challenge that she just had to be a part of it, Trudi smiles, and, as a retired librarian, "Paperback Writer" was the perfect song for her. A technique she used for this quilt is fusible appliqué, which she finds is a quick way to interpret an idea — and this is the first time she has ever used stamping on a quilt.

Besides quilting, Trudi travels, reads, and attends plays, ballets, modern dance performances, and concerts. Occasionally, she also teaches computer classes.

Cotton fabrics, fusible web, scrapbook ephemera, a penny; raw edge and reverse appliquéd, machine-pieced and free motion quilted.

Although she is not "one of their screaming fans," Judy enjoys many of the Beatles' songs. As a teen, Judy learned to play the piano. She still enjoys playing, even though she isn't as good as she used to be. She mostly listens to piano, symphony, and Christian music. It cheers her up, calms her down, or helps her to have a good cry when she needs one.

Her first sewing adventure was when she was eight years old. Judy says she used to watch her mom sew and begged to be taught. Between her mom and her grandmother, she had two very good teachers. She selected "Penny Lane" because she loves the beat. She carefully listened to it, over and over, and the beat of the music and the words to the song gave her the inspiration she needed. This little quilt gave her an opportunity to try different techniques she hadn't attempted before. For her first art quilt, Judy says this piece "was a blast to make!"

Besides quilting, Judy enjoys sight-seeing, biking, boating, bird-watching, gardening, cooking, caring for animals, star-gazing, painting, and cross-stitching. She was a logistics analyst, but when her son, Shane, was born twenty-six years ago, she became a housewife and stay-at-home mom. She looks forward to the next challenge and rearranging her sewing room, since now she needs to share it with her husband, Tom, who also participated in the challenge.

Shannon Gingrich Shirley • Woodbridge, Virginia

Cotton fabric, embroidery floss; needle turn appliquéd, hand-embroidered, free motion quilted, finished with mitered-edge facing.

Shannon is not a Beatles fan *per se*, since she mainly listens to country music, but she enjoys their music. She has been sewing for as long as she can remember — her mum had always done a variety of handwork — and she got her first sewing machine when she was eight years old. From the age of ten to thirteen, she lived in England, where school girls were expected to learn a variety of hand-sewing skills. She loved it! She started quilting in 1998 and was self-taught until 2004, when she started taking technique classes and her quilting changed from all traditional to art quilts using a wide variety of methods.

Shannon is an eclectic quilter who uses a wide variety of techniques in her quilts. She rarely does needle turn appliqué, but she used the technique here because it suited the project. Before she began this quilt, Shannon completed a book manuscript and a magazine article. This left only a week and a half to complete the quilt and turn it in on time, but she did it!

Shannon's quilts have won a number of local and national awards. She feels very lucky to be able to travel and share her quilts with other quilters. The enthusiastic response she gets when she lectures and does trunk shows and workshops is what inspires her on a regular basis. She has published three books with Schiffer Publishing, Ltd. — *Creating Children's Artwork Quilts*, *Let's Get Creative with Quilt Labels*, and *Celebrate the Day with Quilts* — and has been a contributing artist to some of their other art quilt books. She has also had articles appear in numerous magazines.

Shannon worked in retail management at Woodward and Lothrop. She retired when her second daughter was born, and she appreciates that she was able to be a stay-at-home mom for twenty-one years. During that time, she volunteered in all of her daughters' schools and activities.

"PLEASE MR. POSTMAN"

Dolores Marcinkowski • Fairfax, Virginia

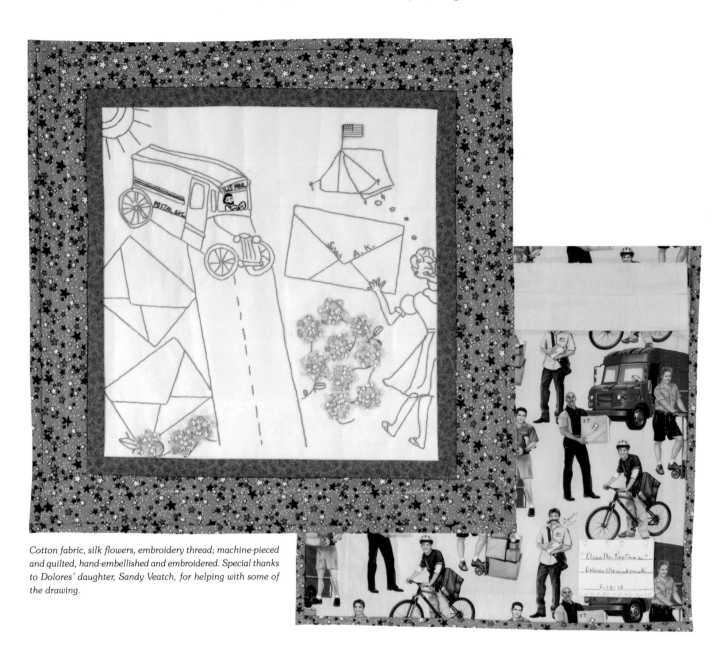

Cotton fabric, silk flowers, embroidery thread; machine-pieced and quilted, hand-embellished and embroidered. Special thanks to Dolores' daughter, Sandy Veatch, for helping with some of the drawing.

Dolores says she is "somewhat" a Beatles fan. She remembers seeing them on TV for the first time and thinking, "Wow, they are different!" Nowadays, she listens to a wide mix of music: oldies, country, and current pop. Music makes her happy.

Dolores selected "Please Mr. Postman" for this challenge because she likes the song. It also reminded her of the mail truck during the Vietnam era. Her husband, Frank, spent well over two years in Vietnam. During that time, the many letters that went back and forth between them meant everything, as there were no computers or cell phones in those days. "Each morning, I wondered if I would get a letter from him," she explains. If she did, it made her day.

Some of the "waiting wives," as they were called, would sit on the curb and wait for the mail truck. If one of them didn't get a letter that day, she recalls, the other wives would console her and say the next day would be better.

Dianne Mehlinger • Arlington, Virginia

Cotton fabric, polythene plastic bags, fiber reactive dyes, potato dextrin; dyed fabric, raw edge appliquéd, and machine-quilted.

Dianne confirms she is "absolutely" a Beatles fan. She saw *A Hard Day's Night* in London in 1964. She sat in the darkened foreign theater and had an amazing cinematic experience that ended with "God Save the Queen." She became a lifelong fan.

Dianne grew up watching her mother and aunts sew clothes and bead sweaters. Her grandmother crocheted bedspreads and doilies. Dianne has been sewing since she was eight years old when her mother enrolled her in a summer sewing class, in which she had to make a shirt and a dress. The dress style back then had a waistline and sleeves, so this was quite an undertaking. She took mandatory home economics in the eighth grade and made an apron and a muumuu. She has been sewing ever since.

Dianne enjoys working with fiber and fabric. This was her first art quilt, and she has plans to make more. Dianne says the idea of a fiber art Beatles quilt appealed to her because she loves their music. She chose "Polythene Pam" because she liked the alliteration of the title. This song contains a great story and some nonsense, too; the nonsense is what most appealed to her, she reveals.

Although the song seems whimsical and simple — the verses are few and short — the music is actually complex with great parts for the guitar and drums, Dianne explains. She wanted to use a psychedelic background with a figure in polythene garb, according to the lyrics. She used the first figure she painted because it was androgynous: mysterious yet happy. The background is a homage to the *Abbey Road* album cover. She listened to a lot of the Beatles' music while working on the quilt and realized she didn't know the songs by title. She hadn't heard some of them in a long time and found it was a great way to pass the time.

Lois still has several of the Beatles' albums and mourned the death of John as a tragic waste. She thinks Paul is a musical genius. She spent many summers in her tween and teen years with her best friend, Margie, listening to the Beatles. "We wrote down the lyrics, committed them to memory, and tried to play the songs backwards on my record player to discover the hidden meanings," she recalls.

Lois comes from a musical family; her German grandparents played several instruments and were entertainers. She played piano briefly and then studied the accordion and voice. Today, music is a vital part of her life. She listens to the radio and her CDs much of the time; she prefers contemporary Christian and classical while at work and quilting, '60s music while cruising, and country and opera in between.

Lois has been sewing for well over fifty years. Her grandmother was a master dressmaker and she taught Lois how to sew on her treadle machine, embroider, and knit. Because she is fairly tall, Lois had difficulty getting the correct fit of garments that were long enough — and this became a great incentive to sew her own clothes.

This is only the second art quilt Lois has made. Though she enjoys and appreciates art quilts, she isn't quite sure "my brain works this way." Since she has just a limited amount of time to devote to quilting, she finds her priority is given to traditional quilts.

Lois chose the song "P.S. I Love You" because "I knew the words and

Cotton fabric and threads; trapunto, raw edge machine-appliquéd and quilted.

melody and had a flash of inspiration." While making this quilt, she considered all of the love letters sent through the ages. She thought about receiving a letter, especially in times of war or hardship, holding it close, and re-reading it. A letter carries the scent of the sender, it was touched by their hands, and was deliberately written and sent just to the recipient, she describes. Her quilt depicts that special love letter soaring across the countryside to a person who is loved as an opportunity to say, "I love you." Skype, text messages, and other constant electronic communications are quick and modern, but a written letter is always special, Lois believes.

"RAIN"

Susanne Miller Jones • Potomac Falls, Virginia

Batik, cotton fabric, nylon flag material, various beads and rhinestones, ribbon, earring backs, metallic and various threads; machine-appliquéd and quilted, hand-beaded.

Susanne was ten years old when the Beatles first appeared on *The Ed Sullivan Show!* She loved their early songs. Now she listens to many kinds of music: hymns, country, big band, musicals, rock and roll, and jazz. Music connects to her emotions; songs bring back memories, tears, and, many times, turn up the corners of her mouth.

Susanne's grandmother taught her to sew when she was five years old. She made clothing for herself as a teenager and clothes for her own children when they were little. She started quilting by trying to finish a quilt her mother's grandmother had started. It was a grandmother's flower garden quilt and the flowers needed to be reset and quilted.

When she heard about this challenge, Susanne recalls that it sounded like fun. She had always wanted to be involved in this type of project, so she considered the possibilities and, quicker than a blink of the eye, she found out the song "Rain" had recently been abandoned and needed someone to adopt it. "Rain" chose her! The title of the song prompted a picture in her mind of an umbrella in the rain. There were two weeks and two days before the deadline, which is not much time to complete a quilt, especially when she envisioned a great deal of hand-beading.

Susanne has only been quilting for three years. She had fun making a previous quilt and experimenting with mixed techniques. She received a "Judge's Choice" award from Marianne Fons for that quilt and was hooked. The Beatles quilt is her third art quilt.

An elementary school teacher for twenty-five years, Susanne also enjoys cooking, reading, traveling, and knitting. She can't imagine life without fibers and needles. She has done all types of handwork and says she has trouble relaxing without a project in her hands.

"REVOLUTION"

Janet R. Palfey • Fairfax, Virginia

Janet attributes her love for the Beatles to being overly influenced by her babysitters as a young child. "They were cool and to be imitated, so when they were excited about something, I was, too," Janet explains — and they were most-assuredly excited about the Beatles! The music was fun and danceable. As Janet grew older, the Beatles began experimenting with different sounds and instruments, "but each album still contained fun music."

Janet has been sewing since she was in her single digits. She came into quilting in her mid-thirties with a garment-making background, so the idea of buying fabric and building a stash before she had a project was a very strange concept to her. How does she know what quantity of fabric she should purchase? Was she really to cut fabric with a surgically-sharp rotary blade with very young children in the house? She learned the answers to these questions from other quilters.

Newly retired from the military, Janet started swimming for exercise when she met Sandy Veatch. One day after a workout coffee break, Janet showed Sandy a small project from a recent quilting class. Sandy issued an open invitation to come to a Monday quilt bee called "Playgroup." Several weeks later, Janet took up the offer and shares that joining the group has "evolved her" as a quilter. She now does more art quilts than traditional, due to the many challenges issued by group members.

Janet decided this quilt would be inspired by the lyrics without too complex of a design. The unseen artist is changing the world from old-fashioned — duller colors with a bumpy edge — to a more hip world — bright psychedelics with a smoothed-out edge. The construction techniques change from a traditional hand-cut, hand-pieced, hexagonal pattern to a modern rotary-cut, machine-pieced, hexagonal pattern. Janet also notes that the British love to play with their language, so she needed to include that aspect. To depict puns for "be" and "all right," she included four bees (one for each Beatle) and the right angle symbol quilted into the background. Other significant quilting designs are the motif from India on the globe and hearts in the background surrounding the world; "after all, love makes the world go 'round," she states.

Janet is an army veteran paratrooper who volunteers with the Girl Scouts and swims with the USA Masters.

Cotton fabrics, various threads, paint sticks; English paper-pieced, machine-pieced, discharge dyed, hand- and machine-appliquéd, stenciled, machine-quilted to include free motion and programmed stitches.

"ROCK AND ROLL MUSIC"

Regina Grewe • Kamen, Germany

Cotton fabrics; paper-pieced, free motion machine-quilted.

Born in 1953, Regina was a young girl when the Beatles were introduced. She vividly remembers listening, clandestinely, to their songs on her older brother's transistor radio. During those early years, she began to do ballroom dancing in tournaments, complete with tulle dresses. After dancing lessons, the youngsters loved to escape to the discotheque to dance to rock and roll, which was socially frowned upon, and that is how the Beatles' music turned into a symbol for revolution, freedom, first love, and, in combination with the beloved dancing, sheer joy of life. Each time Regina hears a Beatles song, all of the memories and happy emotions of that time arise within her and make her shiver.

In 1999, Regina got hooked on quilting. By chance and because of her interest in the technical aspects of quilt-making, she specializes in paper-piecing. Regina chose "Rock and Roll Music" to depict the strong feelings that the Beatles' music still evokes. Her quilt shows dancing legs and a petticoat skirt, even though this was not fashionable in 1964. It is a natural thing for Regina to make her own paper-pieced designs, as she did when she began this quilt. The black, red, and white fabrics had been in her sewing basket for a while and this seemed like the perfect project for using them, she explains.

Regina says that while she loves appliqué and other techniques, sewing for judged competitions is not her cup of tea. In 2008, she started a small business. Via her German and English website, she offers patterns, tips, and classes. She is a member of the German Patchworkgilde, the American Quilters Society, and the Baltimore Appliqué Society. Her patterns have been published in Europe and overseas and two will soon be published in upcoming issues of *Quiltmaker* magazine.

Sandy Veatch • Springfield, Virginia

Growing up, Sandy's military family moved around quite a bit. Wherever they lived, though, it was important to visit the grandparents in Detroit regularly. Sometimes they would have only a long weekend for an eleven-hour car ride, each way, and they would need to start driving at night, as soon as her dad got home from work, or very early in the morning. The kids would pile into the back of the car. Sandy was the youngest, so she was the lucky one who got to lay down in the back of the station wagon, as this was before seat belts.

Her dad enjoyed finding all kinds of music stations to listen to on the radio. Whatever his mood, he turned up the songs and sang really loud. If it wasn't oldies music, then it was often a Beatles song — and he knew all of the words. Sandy's mom always made fully-prepared meals for the family to eat on the long road trips (including fried chicken). Between her mom's food, her dad's singing, and her cozy place to snooze, the many hours in the car never seemed that long, Sandy recalls. Every once in a while, she still gets the urge to go for a long drive. She enjoys many types of music and flips around the radio dial a lot.

Sandy mostly quilts when she feels stressed. She feels like she can do her best work when the house is quiet early in the morning, before anyone else is awake, or when her three sons are at school and she is home alone. The more tiny pieces there are and the more detailed a project is, the better the therapy, she reports.

This is Sandy's first art quilt. She participated in the challenge just to see if the image "I immediately had in my head for 'Rocky Raccoon' would translate onto fabric as artwork," she explains. She has never been able to draw or paint, so this was a great way to challenge herself. She enjoyed making an actual little book for the Bible, complete with gold cording, and the "Vacancy" sign with a letter missing, as well as using real screening over the windows. While making the quilt, Sandy was busy getting her oldest son, Ricky, ready to go away for his first year of college and this proved to be a diversion to that big milestone. She had to slow down to work on this quilt, giving her a chance to think about things. When it was time to leave for college, Ricky walked around the house and said goodbye to the dog — and goodbye to Rocky!

Cotton fabric, leather, window screening, various threads and trims, Tyvek™; machine-appliquéd, free motion quilted, hand-embellished.

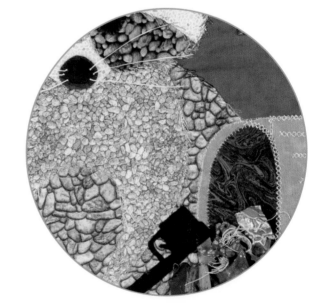

Patricia Dews • Gainesville, Virginia

Cotton fabric, suede cloth, polyester, lace, crushed velvet, buttons;
fusible appliquéd, embellished.

Pat screamed for the Beatles every time they were on TV. She bought all of their record albums in the 1960s and '70s. In February 1964, she gave birth to her son. She didn't find out until he was grown and on his own that he, too, is a huge Beatles fan. She has spent a lot of time searching on ebay™, at estate sales, and in antique stores for vintage Beatles memorabilia for him.

Her grandmother taught her to sew when she was a child, Pat explains, and she won her first sewing contest when she was nine, through a 4-H program. She loves fabric: the touch of it and putting together colors. Quilting is "very forgiving," she states, compared to making clothes. She sews everyday on her machine; at night, she does hand sewing while watching TV.

This is her first art quilt. Pat joined this challenge because she wanted to participate in a group project of this type. Since she is familiar with classical music, "Roll Over Beethoven" called out to her. The first thing she did was to put a 24" x 24" piece of blank paper up on her design wall. It remained blank for at least a month. Pat downloaded the words

to the song and made a list of all of the pictorial words. She cut out images of those words in construction paper and pinned them to the blank paper. She decided to make a large picture of Beethoven, focusing on his haunting eyes. She listened to the song on her computer several times before getting started and then, gradually, she converted everything from paper to fabric. She continued to hear the song in her head while she worked on the quilt.

Pat worked for the Federal government for more than thirty years in financial management. She retired as deputy controller for the Public Buildings Service, General Services Administration. She sells on eBay, plays online poker and Words with Friends™ on Facebook®, bowls, plays Bunco®, and reads. She also makes wearable art, as well as a variety of other things for charity: pillowcases, teddy bears, pillows and totes for cancer patients, bags made to go on walkers, pillowcase dresses for poor children, and quilts. She has won several quilt show and Hoffman Challenge awards. She also consults and makes costumes for a little theater group; for one production, she designed and made over forty outfits.

"SAVOY TRUFFLE"

Nadine M. Duke • Fairfax, Virginia

As a young teenager, Nadine remembers watching *The Ed Sullivan Show* on TV with her mom the night the Beatles were introduced. She had never heard of them and was amazed by their look ("those shaggy manes") and their sound. When they finished singing, Nadine looked at her mom and asked, "What was THAT?!" Nadine also recalls all of the kids talking about the Beatles afterwards; lots of girls at her junior high school in California spent their lunch break writing love stories, featuring themselves and their favorite Beatle.

Nadine's father had a beautiful voice, and she can remember hearing him sing love songs to her mom as he walked home from work. He sang special songs to his daughters, too. Music was always a source of comfort and joy in her home, she explains.

Nadine's mother taught her how to sew clothes and her sister, Jeannine, taught her to embroider and do crewel. Nadine said sewing clothes became less fun when she no longer had a cute figure to show off, but quilting satisfies her love of pretty fabrics. Today, when she finishes a quilt, she often gives it away as a gift. "It says 'I love you' better than anything else I can imagine," she insists. Nadine adds that as the wife of a naval officer, she discovered any place can feel like home once quilts are on a bed.

Nadine suggested to her daughter Heather they each make

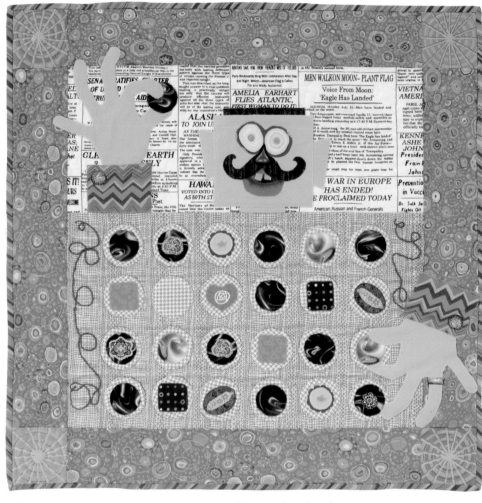

Cotton fabric, embroidery floss; hand-embroidered, machine-pieced, appliquéd, and quilted. Machine-quilted by Pauline Lipscomb of Wicomico Church, Virginia.

a quilt for this challenge because she thought it would be a good mother-daughter experience. Since neither of them had made an art quilt before, it seemed like an exciting opportunity for both of them to try something new. Nadine chose "Savoy Truffle" because she loves chocolates. The song is about the pleasure of enjoying a box of yummy, chocolate bonbons. Other than the song's lyrics, what inspired this quilt were the fabrics themselves, and she had fun finding luscious, molten chocolate fabric and other colorful prints to make the bonbons. She wanted the quilt to be whimsical and kind of silly, as the song suggests. When she saw the fabric with the swirly circle prints, she immediately thought of the sugar-crazed look of her funny guy's eyes. Of course, he has bad, yellowed teeth from eating too many sweets. She remembers her favorite mod dress in the late sixties was striped orange and hot pink, so she wanted those wild colors in her quilt, too. It was a happy revelation for Nadine to learn you don't need to be an artist to make an art quilt — you just have to think like a kid with a bunch of construction paper! She "smiled a lot" during the process of making this quilt, Nadine reveals.

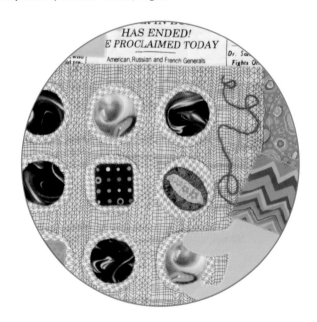

"SEA OF HOLES"

Norma Colman • Berryville, Virginia

While Norma doesn't consider herself a fan, she acknowledges that the Beatles "were a large influence on me," both culturally and artistically. One of the most memorable evenings of her childhood was the night the Beatles appeared for the first time on *The Ed Sullivan Show*. Her family was attending a church social event. The two daughters of the pastor, and all of the other young people who so desired, were allowed to go over to the parsonage to watch the show. Similar permission was never granted again. Even then, Norma recognized "this music group was shaping our culture."

Norma loves that she can read music; it is another language. She continues to sing with pleasure and reverence during church services, and she counts numerous local musicians among her friends. They encourage spontaneous kazoo duets and Norma's famous bourbon dance. It gives her delight that song performances are dedicated to her; music builds community.

Norma started sewing in 4-H in Geneseo, Illinois, where learning to sew was a requirement of farm girls. Her mother would rip out the stitches while Norma cried, but finally it began to make sense. Norma's craftsmanship has always been pretty good, as it is the result of "practice, practice, and more practice," she reveals. Today, she quilts to be able to touch fabric, to create and recreate shape, and to appreciate line, Norma says. She began making church banners and wall hangings as a young adult, but she didn't think of them as art quilts. Years later, several good teachers and a close band of skirted sisters taught her more skills "and encouraged me to claim the title of 'artist.'"

Norma admits she couldn't resist this challenge. "It seemed like a doorway to have some fun in a summer already filled with commitments and commissions," she contends. She loves the imagery of her quilt. Norma has a pioneer spirit, so she wanted this piece to be about daily adventure. She also confessed that for a very long time "I have wanted to make a quilt with the batting showing," so she painted the batting and covered it with window screen. She bought one of her sewing machines for the quality of the buttonholes it made and the ease in doing so. There are fifty buttonholes in this piece. As she attached the binding, she realized "all of the materials I used are part of my daily life" in her studio. She admits she once sought to have "energy and hope in my work. This year my perspective shifted to clarity and complexity," both of which Norma sees in her "Sea of Holes" quilt.

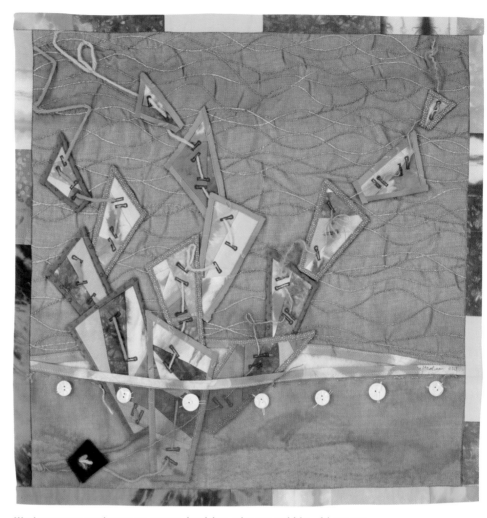

Window screening and casement, cottons, hand-dyes, other assorted fabric, fabric paint, yarn, buttons felt, and batting; machine-pieced, hand-stitched, couched, and embellished.

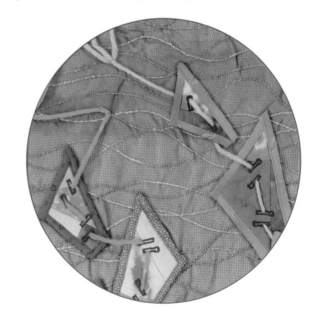

"SGT. PEPPER'S LONELY HEARTS CLUB BAND"

Dianne Harris Thomas • Fairfax, Virginia

Cotton, silk, lamé, tulle, grocery store net produce bags, ribbon, a dress belt, beads; drawn, machine-pieced, appliquéd, and quilted, beaded.

Dianne was a fan of the Beatles' softer songs, especially from the *Rubber Soul* album. She taught herself to play hymns from a church hymnal when she was in middle school and she used to sing in church choirs. Now, she listens mostly to folk-rock and Broadway show tunes. Music lifts and sometimes heals her spirit. Music also distracts her, so while she is doing her creative work, she turns the classic movie channel on TV and listens to the dialogue of 1940s movies. She learned to sew in a middle school home economics class. After that, her mother gave her advice about sewing projects.

Sgt. Pepper's Lonely Hearts Club Band was the first Beatles album Dianne bought. The composition on the album cover always interested her and she thought she might have fun substituting her own drawings of people for the celebrity photos in it. Her typical style of quilting is representational and the freeform quilting on this quilt is a style she often uses. She has been obsessed with making art quilts since she first saw some in 2007. She joined in this challenge because she thought it was a wonderful idea and felt the concept not only gave each quilter her or his own project, but it also produced a cohesive group of quilts.

Dianne was a high school art teacher, a technical writer, and a consulting business owner. She also enjoys reading, table games, and watching sports with her husband. While she made her Beatles quilt, her daughter Dylan's baby, Livia, was born. She is proud one of her quilts was exhibited at the American Quilter's Society Quilt Show in Paducah and two others have been shown at the International Quilt Festival in Houston.

"SHE CAME IN THROUGH THE BATHROOM WINDOW"

Kris Bishop • Woodbridge, Virginia

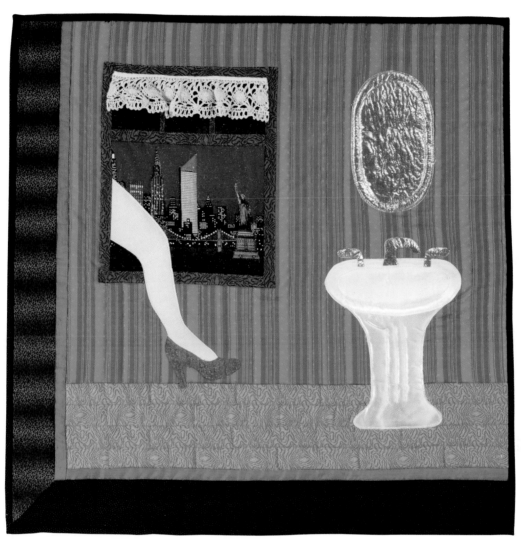

Cotton, silk, satin, lamé, metallic fabric, crocheted lace; raw edge appliquéd and machine-quilted.

Kris graduated from high school in 1966 and grew up with the Beatles. She can remember hurrying home with her sister to watch them the first time they appeared on *The Ed Sullivan Show* and says she is "definitely" a fan. Kris has no musical background, though she loves all types of music, especially the oldies. When she was very young, Kris started sewing by making doll clothes and yo-yo quilts. She has been sewing for sixty years, Kris says, because she enjoys making things and finds sewing to be a relaxing outlet.

Kris grew up listening to "She Came in Through the Bathroom Window" and always loved the lyrics. She immediately pictured the design in her head for this quilt: a wild lady climbing into the bathroom window. She envisioned the porcelain sink and wild high heels, she laughs. However, using such slippery fabrics presented a special challenge. Kris doesn't really have a particular style of art quilting; "I just do whatever suits my inspiration," she maintains.

Kris has participated in numerous challenges, and many of her quilts have traveled and been displayed around the world. Her quilts have also been published in books. She is a retired teacher who enjoys beading, knitting, gardening, reading, and traveling.

"SHE LOVES YOU"

Lisa Chin • Salt Lake City, Utah

Lisa has been a fan of the Beatles since childhood, and their songs have narrated much of her life. She began sewing at a young age, and she continues to learn new skills and techniques from anyone who will teach her, as well as how-to books. Lisa says today's generation of sewers is fortunate to have videos and tutorials at their fingertips any time of day or night. At the urging of a friend, Lisa joined a local quilt guild almost ten years ago. The meetings were filled with fantastic women willing to share their knowledge during weekly and monthly meetings. It was at these meetings that she discovered art quilts, and now, thanks to them, she found a whole new world she is enjoying immensely.

Since she loves the Beatles' music, Lisa is happy to have had the opportunity to participate in this challenge. She chose "She Loves You" because that is the first Beatles song she remembers hearing. Lisa knew the lyrics referred to a love between a boyfriend and a girlfriend, but when she looked through old photos for inspiration, she came across a photo of her mom looking at her as an infant — and she knew she had found the meaning she wanted to portray. "Mom was only nineteen when I was born and I knew she always loved me."

Lisa says the music and lyrics of "She Loves You" were "on a loop in my imagination through the entire process." A few weeks before the quilt

Hand-dyed and commercial cotton fabrics, textile paint, water-soluble crayons; thermofax screen printed; stenciled; fusible appliquéd, thread painted and machine-quilted.

was due, Lisa realized she would be on vacation the week before the deadline, so she needed to get all of her plans in action. She put off washing clothes and packing and shopping for her trip so she could have everything stitched up before they left. Fortunately, her family pitched in with the preparations and together they made it all work. She was able to finish the machine-stitching before the trip. She hand-stitched the binding and sleeve during the ten-hour car ride.

Lisa is married to a man she describes as "wonderfully supportive" and she is mother to one son and three daughters. She is a member of the Utah Surface Design Group, the Utah Quilt Guild, Quilters Holladay, and SAQA. She teaches classes in fabric surface design techniques and improvisational piecing. She has had patterns published in *Quilting Arts Gifts*, *Quilt Scene*, and *Modern Patchwork*, and will soon be published in several books.

"SHE'S LEAVING HOME"

Jodie Flakowicz • Arlington, Virginia

Cotton fabric, embroidery thread, fabric glue, pen and fabric markers; machine-stitched and embroidered.

Jodie says she is absolutely a Beatles fan who was "caught in the wave of Beatlemania, along with the rest of my friends, from the very start." She believes their creativity and innovation changed popular music as we know it, and that it brought about new approaches and methods not used in the past. They also took this popular music to a new level of sophistication, which influenced future musicians for years to come. "They were a major part of my 'formative years' and continue to be a part of who I am," she states. Growing up, she created a Beatles scrapbook, listened to their albums over and over again, and collected Beatles cards. She remembers watching *A Hard Day's Night* and *Help*. "I screamed right along with everyone else in the theater through the entire show," she recalls. Not long ago, she saw a glimpse of *Help* and was tickled to see there was an actual plot to the movie.

Jodie's mother taught her how to sew by hand when she was very young. She did counted cross-stitch and embroidered her jeans when she got older. She had to take home economics in the eighth grade, but her class was not into this at all, as feminism was on the rise. Views of what women could do, beyond traditional roles, were changing. "Our poor teacher didn't know what to do with us ... we challenged her every step of the way, in whatever she was trying to teach," Jodie states.

This is Jodie's first art quilt. She realized she could not pass up the opportunity of this challenge. She chose "She's Leaving Home" because it had a storyline she could easily visualize and she was pleased with the process and how it turned out. "It's like I turned on the more interesting parts of my brain that I hadn't used in years and years to make this quilt," she marvels.

Since the Beatles quilt challenge began, Jodie has joined three fiber groups. This project truly excited her, and she shared her progress with all three groups of women. They have been responsive to her questions and concerns. Best of all, Jodie adds, she realizes how lucky she is to have found these women who are such a warm, giving, positive addition to her world.

"SHOUT"

Andrea L. Harles • Washington, D.C.

When Andrea first heard the Beatles, she wasn't a fan. She says she didn't dislike them, she just wasn't impressed. "I think I was just too fuddy duddy," she laughs. During her first year in college, everything changed.

Andrea's first strong memory involving the Beatles' music was on April 22, 1970: the first observance of Earth Day. She was in Dunn Meadow at Indiana University. Many of the "adults" at the university and in the town considered this new concern for the earth and the environment colossally stupid. Speakers responded to their ridicule. Finally, the speeches were over and, through the speakers, everyone heard the Beatles song "Here Comes the Sun" played loud and strong. It felt very supportive and encouraging, and she has a memory of the sun, indeed, coming out from the clouds, both literally and metaphorically.

Andrea's second memory is from December 1971. While touring the Soviet Union with a group of her Russian language students, she was curious about what was on Soviet Radio and they turned up the volume. She was totally floored when she heard John Lennon singing "Imagine," even though she had heard that the Beatles' music was banned there. This was an eye-opener. It also occurred to her that those in power in the Soviet Union didn't understand what the Beatles were saying any more than anyone else did in the non-communist world.

Vintage Peter Max-style polyester blend and other fabric; fusible machine appliquéd and quilted.

Andrea has been singing in her church choir for more than thirty years. There is a lot to be gained from this experience of discipline, practice, and commitment, she says. There is also the valuable lesson of "joining together to make something that in sum is much greater than the simple contributions of each individual." It teaches her to see patterns much broader, deeper, and more organically and spiritually. Today she listens to popular music, as well as classical, both ancient and modern, and some country that blends into folk or rock. She also enjoys Latin, Russian, Georgian, Celtic, and "just a lot of other weird stuff." Music is the part of her life that enriches, feeds, and challenges her and opens her up to new expression in the creative process. By being willing to engage different and new kinds of music, she is more able to envision and approach her art from an innovative point of view.

Andrea began sewing at the age of four on her great-grandmother's treadle machine. Though she doesn't recall what she sewed, she remembers being fascinated with the machine and the rhythm of the treadle. She has been making art quilts since she was in high school and college, "except I called them banners." It was the 1960s and they were exploring new means of expression, so the freedom and unconcern for rules that is a part of art quilts has always been a part of her quilting. In her quilting, "I am always experimenting and trying new things." Sometimes the things are just new to her and sometimes she is developing a new slant, way, or approach. She loves to design quilts and has more ideas than she is able to do anything with, but she plans to keep working at it.

When Andrea first heard about this project, she was thrilled. Although she didn't realize it at the time, this was just what she had been waiting for. The Beatles were the best part of the '60s. They were revolutionary in a bright way, full of life, writing and singing songs that were tuneful, but also surprising, challenging, had depth of meaning, and often were just fun. They were the "movie score" for this era. This was also the answer for a piece of fabric a friend had given her that she had been saving for years for something special. As she ironed it, she recognized the almost forgotten smell of polyester blends — how appropriate this fabric was to celebrate the Beatles and 1970. She chose the song "Shout" because it was vibrant, "like the Beatles, the era, and my fabric."

"SIE LIEBT DICH"

Linda Marcinowski • Alexandria, Virginia

Cotton fabric, rickrack, fabric paint; raw edge and reverse appliquéd, hand- and machine-pieced, embellished, painted, hand- and machine-quilted.

Linda remembers singing to her transistor AM radio and dancing like crazy to the upbeat tunes of the Beatles. Her parents didn't like the sound of rock and roll music, but Linda couldn't help liking it. Growing up in the San Francisco Bay area in the 1960s, music was everywhere.

Linda learned to play the acoustic guitar when she was ten and loved to strum along to music on the radio. Country music always puts her in a good mood while classical helps her to concentrate. She can't imagine cruising without listening to music. "When I close my eyes and listen to the music, I can see colors pulsating inside my head and the creative ideas just flow," she reveals.

Though she considers herself more of a traditional quilter, Linda likes art quilting because "it's a way of personalizing a piece with unique tidbits of reality." She also finds quilting is relaxing for her. "I like being at peace with my thoughts and creating something beautiful at the same time," she admits. She chose "Sie Liebt Dich" because it reminded her of living in Germany and the fun she had watching the

Beatlemania there. She joined this challenge because she thought it would be fun to do something based on the music of the Beatles. For her inspiration, she imagined a German girl hopelessly in love with a guy who doesn't realize how lucky he is to have her affection. Linda listened to the song in both English and German and thought about the huge cultural impact the Beatles had on society in the 1960s.

Linda became a career military officer's wife, and then her joy was raising two daughters and traveling. Among other things, she has been a newspaper correspondent, a legal secretary, a salesperson, a shop manager, teacher, mentor, family support group facilitator, and she is on the staff of the Jinny Beyer Studio. She has painted store windows for Christmas, designed clothing and gift cards for charity, and made crafts to sell. She attends the International Quilt Festival every year and is always amazed by the things she sees there. "It has been exciting to be involved with the quilting movement as it has evolved," she exclaims.

"STRAWBERRY FIELDS FOREVER"

Jeanne Coglianese • Fairfax, Virginia

Jeanne's earliest memory of listening to music is lying on the floor, on her stomach, in front of her family's 12" black and white TV, watching the Beatles perform on *The Ed Sullivan Show*. She remembers all of the screaming fans.

Jeanne had no formal music training until she retired. "Being retired has given me the time and opportunity to pursue music as more than just a fan," she says. She is in a recorder consort and plays the tenor recorder. She also sings alto in the Encore Chorale group. Music keeps her continually learning new things, improving her skills, and is the focus for social interaction with a great group of retired friends, Jeanne explains.

Jeanne enjoys the community of quilters. "They are a talented, nurturing, encouraging and sometimes hilarious group of friends," she declares, adding that quilting has introduced her to many women from a variety of backgrounds "I would not otherwise have met."

Jeanne only recently started making art quilts. As president of the Fairfax Chapter of Quilters Unlimited, to which several of the challenge participants belong, she likes to support the group by participating as much as possible. She chose "Strawberry Fields Forever" because she thought it would be an easy one for "a beginning art quilter" to represent. She did some research on the song and found Strawberry Field was an actual place where John played with his friends when he was a boy — this broadened her ideas of what the quilt should look like.

Cotton fabric, buttons; hand-appliquéd and quilted, machine-pieced and quilted.

Jeanne and her husband went to Ireland and England in the spring of 2013. When Jeanne learned Strawberry Field was in Liverpool, she checked the itinerary and found out that if they were willing to add another hour or so to a long day of driving, she could visit the site. Just as she and her husband got there, a Magical Mystery Tour bus filled with students from Ohio State pulled up; Jeanne states that it added a lot of excitement to the visit to share this with students. The visit changed what she planned to do for her quilt. Though she kept the background she had already completed, which was a technique she learned by taking a Craftsy® class online by Judith Trager on art quilt backgrounds, she decided to design her own gates to the park. She found inspiration in her stash; the multicolored batik fabrics recalled the tie dyes of the '60s.

Jeanne belongs to a couple of different chapters of Quilters Unlimited and to three knitting groups. She has two mini-quilts in the Smithsonian Museum's permanent collection used to decorate trees at Christmas and she has a quilt in Pat Sloan's *Crooked Cabin Quilts* book.

"SUN KING"

Lynn Chinnis • Warrenton, Virginia

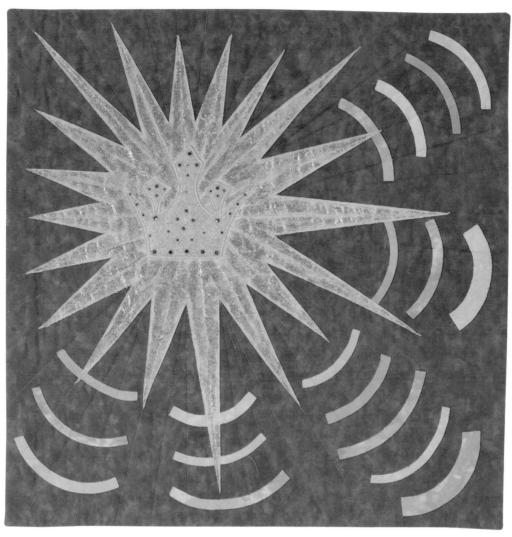

Commercial and hand-dyed fabric, various threads, crystals; fusible raw edge appliquéd, machine-quilted.

Lynn is a Beatles fan who listens to a couple favorite CDs she plays when she is working on her longarm sewing machine. "The rhythm seems to make the quilting go smoother," she says. Though music is often a distraction when she is planning a quilt, she likes to listen to it when she begins working with fabric. She has been sewing since the late 1960s when her husband was still in graduate school in Ann Arbor, Michigan. She made clothing for herself and home decorator items for their townhouse. She sewed clothing for her daughter, Sarah, and she also made a quilt in 1975 for Sarah's first "big girl" bed. She didn't quilt again until 1992, when a friend asked her to take a class with her. By that time, rotary cutters were popular and Lynn was delighted to not need to make templates from old cardboard anymore.

Lynn eventually got bored following traditional patterns, so she decided to take some art classes and art quilting classes. Now, she makes traditional quilts and art quilts. She calls herself a "fiber junkie" because she loves all sorts of fabric, threads, and yarns.

Lynn listened to several Beatles songs and really liked "Sun King." She immediately had an idea of what she would do, "although that isn't the way the quilt finally turned out," she laughs. Having a starting point — whether it is a color, idea, or theme — makes it easier to develop a design, Lynn insists. She tends toward using geometric shapes on calm backgrounds, so this is a pretty typical piece. The lyrics inspired the quilt, she adds, explaining she had read that George had said the sound of "Sun King" was inspired by a Fleetwood Mac song called "Albatross." Lynn had never heard that song before, so she listened to it and discovered the sounds of the early Fleetwood Mac. She ended up listening to a lot of early Fleetwood Mac, British blues groups, and the Beatles while working on her quilt. "When you investigate a theme, it can lead you down a lot of interesting paths, even if the results don't actually end up in the final product," she muses.

"SWEET LITTLE SIXTEEN"

Carole A. Nicholas • Oakton, Virginia

Cotton fabric, beads, buttons, Swarovski crystals; machine-appliquéd, hand-stitched. Special thanks to Starla Phelps, who applied the crystals in Lucy's sky.

Carole's roommate in graduate school at Columbia University during 1966 through 1968 had every Beatles song ever recorded. Carole has two favorite memories of those years: one was meeting cultural anthropologist Margaret Mead in the elevator in Schermerhorn Hall; the other was totally missing the fire hoses and police dogs during the televised sit-in of 1968 because she entered by the back door to defend her thesis. She listened to the Beatles on the stereo in the living room of her rented apartment in Butler Hall while she and her friends talked about beaus who came and went.

"Sweet Little Sixteen" is a quilted celebration of the fiftieth anniversary of the Beatles first appearance in the U.S. Carole remembers crowding into the TV room of her college dorm to watch one of their concerts. She also recalls their appearance on *The Ed Sullivan Show*. The sixteen cupcakes each represent specific Beatles songs (even more are depicted on the reverse side). Here are the individual songs that decorate each cupcake, from the top row, left to right: "Birthday" and "When I'm 64," "All You Need is Love," "Carol," "Piggies," "She's Leaving Home," "Ticket to Ride," "Hey Jude," "Drive My Car" and "I'll Follow the Sun," "Money" and "Penny Lane," "Good Day Sunshine," "Too Much Monkey Business," "Blackbird," "I Want to Hold Your Hand," "I'm Happy Just to Dance With You," "Strawberry Fields Forever," and "Sgt. Pepper's Lonely Hearts Club Band." "Lucy in the Sky With Diamonds" floats across the top of the quilt. The reverse side of the quilt includes "Yellow Submarine," "Across the Universe," "Octopus's Garden," and "Lady Madonna."

"TAXMAN"

Ellen Brereton Icochea • Alexandria, Virginia

Cotton, embossed suede, microsuede, wool suiting, polyester, vinyl, crystals, mother of pearl buttons; drawn, printed fabric, hand- and machine-appliquéd and pieced. Special thanks to Laura Hernandez, Ellen's niece, for creating the tax percentage line graph.

When Ellen started this project, she didn't really have a Beatles story. This changed in July 2013, when she went to the local post office to mail birthday presents. The postman asked if she wanted to hear about the best birthday present he ever received, and proceeded to tell her how when he was eighteen his father was on the board of the D.C. Stadium. He obtained two tickets for his son and high school sweetheart to attend the Beatles concert. Says Ellen, "The postman stood there, so many years later, with a huge smile on his face, remembering that concert." Even though he said he was in the nosebleed seats, he described it as loud, full of energy, and "one of the best nights of his life." And what was the price to be a witness to musical history? Two dollars apiece.

Some of Ellen's earliest and happiest memories of time spent with her father are those that include music. On Saturdays and Sundays, during her childhood and teenage years, her father often gave her a little money. They would sneak out of the house and spend a couple of hours in the music section of a store browsing and purchasing 45s, LPs, and later eight tracks, cassettes, and CDs. On some weekends, her family would walk along Beale Street in Memphis to listen to the blues musicians, such as Ma Rainey and B.B. King.

Ellen has always used music to celebrate life with family and friends, and she has long enjoyed singing in the car, shower, and church. However, in 2012, it became a critical part of her cognitive recovery from brain surgery. Her neurosurgeon, Dr. Fraser Cummins Henderson, Sr., instructed her to learn either a complex foreign language or to learn to read and play music in order to recover her math skills post-surgery for Arnold Chiari Malformation of the brain (a birth defect that can cause problems with balance and coordination). Ellen chose to learn music and play the Appalachian mountain dulcimer. Since she started playing the dulcimer, her ability to balance her checkbook has increased. In addition, through classes and music jam sessions, she has met wonderful people whom she would not have met otherwise.

This is Ellen's first art quilt. Though art quilting is what initially attracted her to quilting, she felt she needed to learn how to sew in the traditional way before she attempted art quilting. Ellen states she quilts as a creative outlet and expression as much as she does for the friendships. She has always worked in male-dominated fields and didn't have many female friends — until she discovered this interest.

Ellen chose the song "Taxman" because she found it amusing and interesting on many levels. Yearly, in both the United Kingdom and the United States, "we hear the sarcastic and angry refrain over the radio and loud speakers in the post office," as tax filers try to beat the taxman's deadline, she muses. Coincidentally, Ellen was shocked to find out that by 1965, George was in the United Kingdom's ninety-five percent tax rate. As for the inspiration for this quilt, after learning George was influenced by the *Batman* series in writing this song, she decided to portray the taxman as a villain in cartoon format.

As she continues to work on her medical recovery, Ellen says she feels blessed to be surrounded by a wonderful husband, family, and friends. Before her surgeries, she was a senior executive with the FBI. She also worked for America Online and MCI Telecommunications. She has earned several awards throughout her career. The most personally meaningful one was awarded in October 2008, when she won the Federal Bureau of Investigation Security Distinguished Career Service Medal. Ellen is actively engaged in three charities related to her medical condition, and she loves reading biographies and traveling and doing photography with her husband.

"TELL ME WHAT YOU SEE"

Kurt DeSoto • Fairfax, Virginia

*Microsoft Office®, Adobe® Acrobat®, QR Droid™, Dell™ desktop PC;
cut and pasted, sized, formatted, layered, colorized, cropped, saved.*

When Kurt was young, he used to sing Beatles tunes to soothe his childhood anxieties. He especially remembers singing "I Want to Hold Your Pan" when he helped his mom cook blueberry pancakes for dinner. He was disappointed to learn the real words…until he met his wife. Now she makes him pancakes to soothe his adult anxieties; their agreement is he, for the most part, doesn't sing, though he loves all kinds of music. The creativity in music inspires him to be creative, too, Kurt says. More recently, he enjoys listening to the music his children make: his son, Andy, plays the piano and the tuba and his daughter, Aimee, the clarinet and ukulele.

Kurt began sewing out of necessity, either when a button fell off a shirt or when a toe poked out of a favorite pair of socks, he explains. Although his wife sews, she tells him she doesn't do "that kind of sewing." He jokes that if he didn't sew, he would hold his hand over his shirt where the missing button is.

This virtual quilt is his first quilt. Kurt became interested when he realized he could design it with QR codes. He chose this particular song because quilts, like most art, require interaction and interpretation by the viewer. The QR codes would encourage such activity, as many people have a QR reader app on their smartphone and they can scan a code on his virtual quilt, linking them to a website he created with information about the song's (and the quilt's) underlying theme.

More specifically, Kurt notes, the lyrics to the song suggest overcoming negatives (the black clouds) by "entrusting your heart" and "opening your eyes" to the "surprise" offered by another. These lyrics are depicted by four large QR code squares of four principal colors with four shapes beneath the codes, each representing one of the four key elements in the song that Kurt also associates with a particular Beatle. Paul is represented by the red square with the underlying heart, symbolizing love; John is symbolized by the black QR code with threatening clouds underneath, since he raised issues about social awareness and injustice; the blue square with the eyes refers to George, who was spiritual and contemplative; and the green square represents Ringo. Kurt thinks of Ringo as the fun-loving Beatle, full of surprises. In that vein, the shape below Ringo's green square is the familiar optical illusion with the faces and vases. Kurt hopes visitors to his website will appreciate "what they see."

"THE CONTINUING STORY OF BUNGALOW BILL"

Dorry Emmer • Great Falls, Virginia

Cotton fabrics, beads; appliquéd, hand-embroidered, pieced, machine quilted. The work of others inspired parts of this quilt: the 2013 mystery quilt by Reiko Kato inspired the children, and the concept for this Sunbonnet Sue and Overall Andy came from the Australian book 501 Quilt Blocks.

Dorry was at boarding school in New Zealand in the late 1960s, and the only time students were permitted to have their transistor radios was on the weekends. They sunbathed on beach towels in the tennis court area and listened to the "Top Ten" hits each week. The list was always dominated by the Beatles. She is less of a fan now than she was a few decades ago, but when she wakes up in the wee hours of the night she sings songs in her mind to distract her from dark thoughts. One song that makes a frequent appearance on her singing playlist is "Ob-La-Di, Ob-La-Da."

Dorry didn't instinctively know this particular song, but she discovered it was on *The White Album*, a favorite of her late husband. "I guess I was sort of making this as a memorial to him," she acknowledges. Their son, Geoff, is always happy to provide suggestions whenever she asks and she's grateful to him for providing that input on this challenge piece and for cheering her on. She hopes it is obvious this quilt was inspired by the song title. She tried to depict aspects from the lyrics rather than the meaning behind

them. She never made a quilt before featuring Sunbonnet Sue, but she wanted to have a little fun with the much-maligned Sue, who, she claims, has an undeserved bad reputation as a fuddy-duddy. When she found the tiger stripe fabric, she bought it right away for the finishing touch, which would be the binding. After all, the song is about hunting tigers!

Dorry began quilting when she moved to the U.S. in 1980. She explains that she wanted to do something to help break the ice with her American mother-in-law who made simple quilts, so she took a beginner quilt class. She quilts now because "I like to be creative and try new things." She also loves the camaraderie of being with other quilters. "Quilting has gotten me through some difficult times in my life," Dorry confides.

An award-winning quilter, Dorry also curates exhibits and participates in a variety of quilt groups, including one that makes quilts to present to wounded U.S. service personnel.

"THE END"

Barbara Hollinger • Vienna, Virginia

Cotton fabric; hand-appliquéd and machine-quilted.

When asked if she is a Beatles fan, Barb's quick response was, "Of course I am! Aren't we all?" Her first slow dance with an "actual boy" was to the song "Let It Be" as it played in her junior high school gym — a moment she will never forget.

Barb joined the school band in the fifth grade, but did not want to sit in the woodwinds section with the silly girls. Instead, she played the trombone, but was too short to reach the slide to its furthest extension. She had to fling the slide out, catch the end with her foot, and then kick it back once the note was played. Since then, any music featuring a brass section gets her attention.

Barb decided to participate in this project because, she laughs, "I can't say 'no' to a good challenge." She adds that she chose the song "The End" because "I like to have the final word in any discussion." While she drew out the design, she put the song on repeat. She hoped to capture the rhythm of the song in her design. Now she can't get the beat out of her head.

Schooled as an engineer, Barb still thinks and acts like one. In her next lifetime, she muses, she will be able to draw and paint with the skill and talent of the masters, but for now, she quilts. She loves making something of beauty and function where there once was none. Her hands are happiest when they are rearranging, repairing, repurposing, constructing, and creating; the materials involved don't really matter. She is a member of Studio Art Quilt Associates and Fiber Artists @ Loose Ends. She has been published in the book *Great American Quilts*, was a frequent contributor to *Machine Quilting Unlimited* magazine, and was also the curator for the Sacred Threads Exhibits in 2011 and 2013.

"THE HIPPY HIPPY SHAKE"

Sarah Lykins Entsminger • Ashburn, Virginia

Cotton, wool, ultrasuede, vintage buttons, Swarovski crystals, and German glass beads; machine-pieced and quilted, hand-appliquéd and beaded.

Sarah enjoys the Beatles music; most of the songs she knows are playful, happy, and upbeat. She learned to play the violin and piano while she was in school, but sadly lost her ability to play either instrument well over time.

"A small group of wonderful women at my church first taught me to quilt entirely by hand," Sarah reveals. Quilting, she says, is both therapy and a much needed creative outlet. She is drawn to quilting as an artistic expression in a way no other art medium has called to her or allowed her to experiment with different materials and techniques in the same place.

When Sarah heard about this challenge, it seemed like an adventure. The song "The Hippy Hippy Shake" jumped right off the page and into her imagination. She could immediately see girls in Go-Go boots, dancing and shaking around in a party atmosphere.

Sarah's mother thought she was too young to have Go-Go boots when they were all the rage, but older girls who got to wear them seemed to have a lot of fun. She couldn't wait to get a pair of her own, but by then fashions had changed and those dreadful elephant leg polyester pants had become popular. This quilt let her create her own "Go-Go" girls and dress them up for a party. Since it was her party, she could decorate the dance floor in bright, cool colors, which are her favorite, rather than the psychedelic madness of the 1960s.

While imagining a quilt she is about to create, Sarah explains, she needs as quiet a location as possible. Once the sketches begin, the music starts as well. She listens to upbeat music as she works on different elements, especially to keep a focused rhythm as she machine-quilts a piece. While making this quilt, she listened to the *Cello Submarine* CD, a favorite instrumental mix of Beatles' songs by a group of cello players.

149

"THE LONG AND WINDING ROAD"

Jennifer Weilbach • Ashburn, Virginia via Littleton, Colorado

Cotton fabric, batik, various threads, fusible web; machine-appliquéd, machine-embroidered and quilted, hand-embroidered.

As a little girl, Jennifer remembers watching her mom sew living room curtains for vaulted ceilings. She's been hooked ever since. Flash-forward, and she helped her grandma make matching gypsy skirts for her and her sister one Halloween in California. She took home economic classes in junior high and then started making many of her own clothes. Her dad worked in the garment industry in New York (mostly making boys' pants) and brought Jennifer swatch books home to pick fabric from. A few weeks later, a box from the plant in Georgia arrived just for her with her yardage. She made the coolest jumper from a heavy-duty, denim-type fabric with city names in bright colors on a white background. In 1984, she made clothes for her six-week trip to Europe (with her hotel and restaurant services management program in college) because she could only take one small duffel bag and she wanted all of the pieces to coordinate. After she returned, she swiped

her mom's sewing machine, moving it to Denver with her. She still has the 1960, top-of-the-line Singer her mom received as a wedding gift.

Jennifer went to see Paul McCartney in concert during the summer of 2013, during which he played "The Long and Winding Road." The concurrent video montage showed the windswept plains and the mountains. "Purple mountain majesty" isn't just a song lyric, or a quilting pattern, or a string of words … it is Jennifer's life. It's her vision when she took her kids to school, bought groceries, or drove home from anywhere, in any season, at any time. It is her backbone, her homing beacon. Her house is less than a mile, as the crow flies, from the start of "them thar hills," and while she grew up on the ocean's edge in New England and considers all things ocean her soul, the mountains of Colorado are purely the rest of her. So yes, this long and winding road leads directly to her door somewhere in her mountains, somewhere deep inside of her.

150

Joyce Bounds • Annandale, Virginia

Cotton and silk fabric, crystals, buttons, and beads; machine-appliquéd and pieced, hand-appliquéd, hand-embellished.

Joyce loves the Beatles, as do many of her friends. She calls them "the boy band of her youth" and says nothing else compares. She remembers sitting in front of the TV, waiting for *The Ed Sullivan Show* to begin. She screamed along with all of the other girls and knew every single line of every one of their songs. She took piano lessons, but her teacher wouldn't let her play any popular music. She enjoys listening to soft rock now because she has discovered it soothes the soul. When she is being creative, music makes her dance to the beat and work faster.

Joyce has been sewing for ten years. She wanted to learn how to quilt, so she took private lessons for a year from a true master quilter and then joined a guild. She quilts for fun, as well as for the company of other quilters. She can do designs and color a lot better than she can do "exact." When she is making art quilts, "I get to go outside the box and don't have to stay in the lines," she declares.

Joyce chose "The Sheik of Araby" because "the song always made me laugh." She also used to dance to it. Her inspiration made her wonder how you would ever find the sheik in modern times. Her typical style is rather last-minute; she met the deadline, but also took every shortcut. She listened to the Beatles while working on her quilt and shares that even though she isn't a great quilter, "the important thing is to just do the design and then finish it. You don't have to follow the rules!"

Before she retired, Joyce was an ICU nurse manager for thirty years and then an executive manager. If she didn't quilt, she says, "I would do more stained glass."

Trisch Price • Overland Park, Kansas

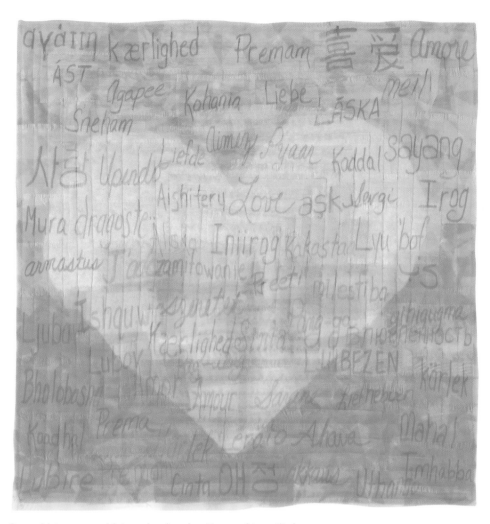

Cotton fabric, organza, fabric marker; frayed, writing, machine-quilted.

While Trisch likes the Beatles and appreciates their music, "I don't really consider myself fanatical."

Trisch has been sewing on and off for thirty-five years. She began in an eighth-grade sewing class. She started quilting twenty years ago when she was working as a computer programmer and going to graduate school for software engineering at night. "I needed to do something that didn't involve a computer," she says. Now she quilts because "it allows me to express my artistic side while making functional items ... I have always doodled and sketched, so making art quilts was just a natural evolution."

The first quilt guild Trisch joined was Quilters Unlimited in northern Virginia. She moved to the Kansas City area about fifteen years ago, but she stays in touch with her Virginia quilting friends. She found out about this challenge through the guild's newsletter. Generally speaking, "I have a hard time passing up a challenge," she admits. She also felt the challenge was a great way to stay connected with friends in Virginia.

Trisch joined the challenge later than most. She took the list of songs available and started searching YouTube; "The Word" was her favorite of those remaining, and she says that "love" inspired her quilt. It is made with overlapping pieces of organza, each with the word "love" written in a different language. She makes modern quilts with an artistic foundation, and likes quilts that require a second look to take in the entire design. The layering in this quilt is typical of her style. She made this piece during the summer when her kids were at home; most of the work was done at the kitchen table. She didn't have the music on, but the song was playing constantly in her head. In order to make the quilt, she put off finishing the last few quilts for her first book. She enjoyed the break this provided to do something different, and she plans to do another challenge quilt next for the Kansas City Modern Quilt Guild. She belongs to the Blue Valley Quilters Guild and was a contributor to the recent book *Classic Modern Quilts* by Jennifer Dick.

Trisch concludes that if she didn't sew, "I would be involved in another artistic endeavor — watercolor painting, home decorating, pottery…who knows!"

"THREE COOL CATS"

Jane M. Brown • Burke, Virginia

Jane's first daughter, Michelle, was named after a Beatles' song. Jane and her husband were trying to come up with a girl's name while on a car ride and the song "Michelle" started playing on the radio. "Harry said, 'I like that name for a daughter,'" she reveals.

Jane grew up in a family of musicians. Her great-grandmother, grandmother, mother, and four siblings were all church organists. Jane took piano and organ lessons from the age of seven into her college years and says she still finds it relaxing to sit down and play the piano once in a while.

Jane was interested to find out what art quilting was all about, so she took a class. There she made many new friends "who became mentors and shared their knowledge and laughter with me." She quilts, Jane contends, "because I have to prove to my husband there is a reason I have a stash of fabric." She also enjoys making quilts as gifts for close relatives and good friends.

Jane chose the song "Three Cool Cats" because "I thought I might be able to make some semblance of an art quilt with the topic and then eventually gift it to my daughter, who owns three cats," she explains. When she thinks of a "cool dude," she thinks of someone with sunglasses. She looked for cartoon depictions of cats that fit the concept of what she wanted to convey. She saw a caricature of just a pair of sunglasses with the main features of a cat — bingo! — and then her thought was to depict a pair of wire-rimmed glasses like she remembers John and Yoko wearing. A

Cotton fabric, screening; fused appliquéd, machine-pieced and quilted. Special thanks to Jane's nephew, Jeff Schweikart, who designed the third pair of sunglasses. Inspiration for other glasses came from clip art of sunglasses with cat-like features.

second pair were reminiscent of sunglasses popular in the 1960s, and the third pair she found in her nephew's animated cartoon and got his permission to use the style because she thought they were cool. On the side panels of the quilt, she quilted a three-cat head to emphasize her song title. While making this quilt, she was visited by her two daughters and granddaughter, who all live out of the area, and put her own quilt on hold while her daughters created their Beatles quilts at her home.

Jane is a mathematician, cartographer, and computer scientist, whose entire career was spent with military mapping agencies. Her duties ranged from actually creating maps to analyzing data with geographic information systems to system administration of security and mail servers for her agency. "It was very rewarding work," she reveals. Retired now, she enjoys musical performances at the Kennedy Center and Wolf Trap Farm Park. In her spare time, she volunteers making Project Linus quilts for disadvantaged children.

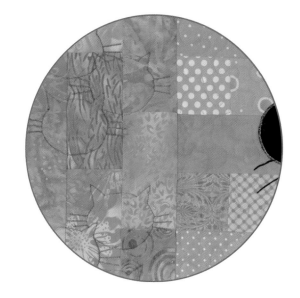

"TICKET TO RIDE"

Paula Rubinoff • Oakton, Virginia

Cotton fabric, various embellishments; transfer printed, hand- and machine-pieced, appliquéd, and quilted.

Paula saw the Beatles in 1964 at Dodger Stadium in Los Angeles and has been a fan ever since. She played the acoustic guitar as a teenager and reveals she most enjoys listening to the music of her youth.

Paula has been sewing since 1993; she got started by watching quilting shows on television. She quilts for an artistic outlet, she maintains, though it also "gives me an opportunity to hang out with other quilters." Although she doesn't consider herself an art quilter, she makes quilts with intricate designs, usually geometric, often from her own patterns or modified patterns of others. This quilt challenge "struck me as something really fun to do," she says, explaining that she chose "Ticket to Ride" because she had "ticket" fabric in her stash. She was inspired by the song title. She already had an amusement park quilt

on her "quilts to do" bucket list; also on her bucket list was a quilt in the style of fiber artist Linda Cantrell. This is the first time she has made a "landscape" quilt or used transfer printing and wire embellishments. She enjoyed infusing a sense of humor in the quilt; she also included a number of Beatles references throughout — see if you can find them all!

Paula was a chief financial officer who started out doing needlepoint and crochet before she began quilting. She has taught classes on beginning paper piecing and easy cathedral windows, and she hopes to develop her own quilt patterns and teaching CDs. She has had quilts juried into the Lancaster and Mid-Atlantic Quilt Festivals, and her blue and white "Basket Weave" quilt was displayed at the Virginia Quilt Museum.

"TILL THERE WAS YOU"

Vanessa McCallum • Germantown, Tennessee

As son... ...songs tran... ...time to the ... ...in junior hig... ...substantial pa... ...her friends, so ... ...the Beatles, "I thin... ...people and places I might otherwise forget." Today, she listens to groups like the Kingston Trio, Queen, and U2, along with the more modern songs of Coldplay and The Killers.

Vanessa finds it hard to sit still while listening to good music, so whether it's a tapping finger, a bobbing head, or an entire dancing body, something has to move. However, that "can interfere with sewing perfect quarter-inch seam allowances," she laughs, adding, "The poetry of a song can take you places, vicariously inserting you in front of a cool breeze or in a war zone. You can feel life through the eyes of others when you listen to a well-written song."

In college, Vanessa took both studio art and art history. By the time she started her first "crazy" quilt in 2006, she had been doing traditional quilting for fifteen years. Crazy quilting was the perfect canvas for all of the artistic techniques she had studied, Vanessa explains.

The song "Till There Was You" gave her an instant grasp of how she could illustrate the emotion of the song as a pictorial crazy quilt. When she thought of the words to the song, she wanted to avoid the obvious and direct connections between what is depicted on the quilt and the words from the lyrics. For instance, there is a church on the hill, but the bells are implied.

Silk, muslin, cotton floss, beads, spangles, paint sticks; machine foundation pieced, hand-embroidered, painted, and stenciled, stump work.

Vanessa had a very busy spring while this quilt was in process. She gave lectures, finished works for a textile show, celebrated her sons' graduations from law and graduate school, and visited mothers in other states. She loves the connection to family she feels when she quilts. Fortunately, her two sons seem to appreciate the quilts she has made for them. She uses quilting as an art form to celebrate milestones: birthdays, graduations, and places she has visited. She hopes future generations treasure her creations as art, as well as the family tradition her stitches capture.

Vanessa is a member of Uncommon Threads Quilt Guild, Memphis Sewing Guild, Fiber Junkies Art Quilt Bee, and Quilters Gone Wild. She has had quilts exhibited in The Wings Cancer Foundation Gallery in Memphis, in the "Healing Elements" and "All Things Bright and Beautiful" exhibits, and at "Quilts and Textiles" at The Arts and Science Center in Arkansas.

"TOMORROW NEVER KNOWS"

Diane Herbort • Arlington, Virginia

Diane describes herself as a "card-carrying Beatlemaniac." The Beatles exploded onto the scene when she was in junior high school, so they grew and changed together. Every album, as well as every single song, has a distinct memory attached because it all truly was the soundtrack of her growing-up years. In our time of a zillion cable TV channels, Internet, and YouTube, it is impossible for anyone born in the last thirty-five years to understand the anticipation of those weeks before the Beatles appeared on *The Ed Sullivan Show*, Diane contends. "We listened to our little transistor radios, we scrutinized the photos on the album and the sleeves of the 45 rpm singles, and we waited," she relates. Who can explain Beatlemania? The music was great. They really could sing and play. They had charm and wit. Diane maintains that every generation wants and needs its own music. "Boy, were we lucky in what we got!" she exclaims.

There was a music/fan magazine called *Sixteen*. They had a contest to write about who was your favorite Beatle and why. Diane wrote about Paul — and, yes, she won the contest! The prizes included Beatles trading cards, a silver ID bracelet with his name on it, and an autographed photo of Paul. She saw the Beatles — twice! She remembers waiting with a couple of school friends outside Cincinnati Gardens. There was a crush of girls, and it was hot, both outside and inside. No one heard

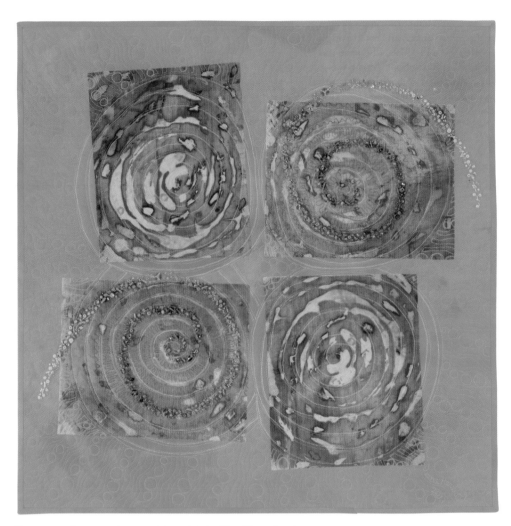

Deconstructed screen prints on cotton printed with cold reactive dyes, hand-dyed cotton, glass beads, sequins, rayon and fluorescent thread; fusible appliquéd, free motion quilted, hand-embellished.

a thing except "EEEEEEEEEEEE!" Thousands of teenagers were screaming. Everyone who was a full-fledged adult, or a male, or anyone who wasn't there, asked and still asks, why all of the screaming? Girls were always told to be quiet and polite, to "behave." The screaming actually was a tiny, but *very loud*, demonstration of independence, of literally finding their own voices. There's an irony in the fact these girls had to gather in a huge mass of young teenager fandom to feel confident and safe enough to do something that might seem a bit rebellious, something with the slightest whiff of misbehavior about it. This was the very first time Diane was sure there were lots and lots of others who felt and thought the same way she did, and this was comforting for a struggling teen. It was the beginning of a sense of belonging that helped them all navigate the next few growing up years.

"I actually touched Paul McCartney!" Diane gushes. It was August 21, 1966, a Sunday morning, and the Beatles' last trip to the U.S. included a performance at the old Cincinnati Reds Stadium. On the day of the concert, a downpour soaked the raised stage and there was

a genuine risk of electrocution. The Beatles were rescheduled for the next day. Somehow, Diane and her two friends talked her mother into driving them to the Netherland Hilton, where the band was staying. They were sure the big black limousine parked out front was a decoy, so they lurked around the back, along with maybe twenty or thirty other fans. Suddenly, a few extra police officers appeared. The limousine pulled up, a door burst open, and a group of eight or ten people came out of the building. They were walking at a fast clip. The police stood side-by-side and stretched out their arms to make a sort of fence between the girls and the Beatles. "I ducked under the arm of a tall cop, reached out just as Paul trotted by, and made contact with his arm!" Diane exclaims. She remembers the feel of the fabric and of her not being brushed off or repelled by him, and of being pretty stunned afterwards that she did manage to make contact when it was such a momentary and random opportunity. "They came and went in about ten seconds — and then we went to the concert and sat halfway up in the bleachers," she recalls.

"TWELVE BAR ORIGINAL"

Claire Alison Josiak • Calgary, Alberta, Canada

Claire was born and raised in England, in a town only twenty miles from Liverpool, so the Beatles were a big influence on her life. She remembers sitting in front of the telly with her family watching the Beatles perform on the 1960s program *Top of The Pops*. George was Claire's favorite. "I liked his smile and the way he played the guitar," she reveals. She also liked that he was more reserved than the others.

Today, music is still a large part of Claire's life. "It awakens the part of me that gets the creative juices flowing," she admits. "It's as if my creative and fun side are sleeping until I hear music — and then the music opens my mind up to many possibilities."

Claire started to sew when she was ten years old. Her grandma was a seamstress and taught her how to use a treadle sewing machine, how to design and cut out her own patterns, and how to embroider: her greatest love is embroidery. She began to quilt when she was an expat living in Stavanger, Norway. Quilting was something she had been interested in learning and in Stavanger there was an international quilting group. Claire says she learned a lot from those quilters who came together from so many different countries. She finds quilting is relaxing. "If I'm upset or anxious, or just having a bad day, when I sit down to quilt, my problems disappear and I feel happy, relaxed, and content," she explains. "There is comfort in holding a needle."

Hand-dyed fabric and threads, fusible web; fusible appliquéd, hand-quilted and embroidered, machine-quilted.

Claire has so many memories of the Beatles music that when this opportunity arose, she wanted to be sure to take part. She chose "Twelve Bar Original" because she had never heard it before. She has learned quite a bit about this song since then and would like other people to appreciate a song they may not have heard. "Twelve Bar Original" is one of the few songs all four Beatles collaborated on. It was recorded during a jam session at the recording studio. It is an instrumental piece and it is the basis for blues music — anyone who wants to play the blues must first learn these twelve bars of music.

To come up with a design for this quilt, Claire did many drawings. About a dozen sketches were taped to her TV room wall where she could peruse them and choose one, but nothing stood out. One evening, friends were visiting and Ken, a musician, asked her why not just do the twelve bars of music? She got her pencils out again and settled on the design that is shown here in her quilt. She knew she wanted her quilt to be colorful, which is why she chose Laura Wasilowski's hand-dyed fabric.

Claire belongs to a small quilt group in a rural community that has contributed quilts to many causes. Everyone in the group collaborated on a quilt sent to New York City following the 9/11 tragedy, and they sent donations to purchase sewing machines to enable women in South America to earn a living with their sewing skills. Her most rewarding project was helping to restore a seventeenth century tapestry at the Glenboro Museum in Calgary. Her next project is to continue embroidery of the Bayeux Tapesty.

157

"TWIST AND SHOUT"

Sylvia Borschel Lewis • Ephraim, Utah

Batik and cotton fabric; fusible appliquéd and machine-quilted.

Sylvia bought her first Beatles album, *Sgt. Pepper's Lonely Hearts Club Band*, when she was fifteen years old, while visiting family in Hamburg, Germany, in 1975. She still owns that album, as well as *Abbey Road* and a couple of others. She worked at a record distributor for a while in the late 1970s. They featured a different type of music station each weekday, and she learned to appreciate various types of music. She was also able to purchase many record albums with her employee discount. She mostly likes to listen to the oldies station and especially music from the '60s and '70s.

While she was in Germany, her Aunt Anita taught Sylvia to crochet. She got hooked on it, and later started doing some embroidery and cross-stitch. Next, she started knitting, sewing clothes for the kids' Raggedy Ann and Andy dolls, and making curtains and other miscellaneous things. Though she tried to get into quilting several times, it didn't take. In 1994, she joined a wonderful quilt guild in Salt Lake City, where she met a bunch of inspiring women, and she has never looked back. Sylvia quilts, she says, "because I find it comforting to put needle and thread to fabric."

Sylvia's art quilting evolved from traditional quilt-making. While living in California, she was exposed to many art quilters. She joined a couple of small groups and found herself stretching artistically. She chose "Twist and Shout" for this challenge because "I absolutely loved the way it was used in the movie *Ferris Bueller's Day Off*!" she laughs. "This song just makes people happy." Her first idea for the quilt was of couples dancing the twist. She was excited to participate in the challenge because she has been looking for ways to expand her art quilt horizons, Sylvia explains, and she really loved the theme. While working on "Twist and Shout," Sylvia's daughter gave birth to her first child.

Sylvia won a ribbon at the Utah Quilt Guild Show for "Best Use of Color." She has also won ribbons at the annual River City Quilt Guild show, and she has a quilt called "Salt Lake Album" that was published in the book *Forget Me Knots* by Jeana Kimball.

"TWO OF US"

Sarah Ann Smith • Hope, Maine

Commercial batik, artist-dyed cotton, fusible web; photo transferred, fusible collage appliquéd, machine-quilted.

Sarah considers herself a modest fan of the Beatles. She likes many of their songs, but she isn't "a walking encyclopedia" of all things Beatles. When she was in the fourth or fifth grade, a friend's dad worked as a disc jockey at a big San Francisco rock radio station. He had tickets and invited Sarah and her friend to go to the Beatles concert at the Cow Palace. Sarah's mom and dad said no way. Sarah sighs, and says she completely understands now why they didn't want an eleven-year-old at a rock concert, but just imagine being there …

When Sarah was six years old, an older girl in the neighborhood made an apron for Sarah's doll and Sarah became enchanted with the idea of making things. She started sewing garments and was an avid sewer from the sixth grade on. When she discovered quilting at the age of twenty-eight, her life changed. Two of her passions came together: art and sewing. She began making art quilts in 2001. Before then, although she was interested in art quilting, a full-time job as

a U.S. diplomat and motherhood took priority. She took a one-day workshop with quilt artist Joan Colvin and never looked back. "I still remember the feeling of elation from picking up cloth and scissors and cutting freely," she smiles.

Sarah chose the song "Two of Us" because it spoke to her about the thirty plus years she and her husband have spent together. She has had this quilt in her head since their thirtieth anniversary, and this song meshed perfectly. It is typical of her style: fused collage and beautiful machine-quilting.

For Sarah, quilting is "as essential to my life as breathing and hugging my kids." An award-winning quilter — she took second prize at the International Quilt Festival — she is the author of the book *ThreadWork Unraveled*. She has also written several articles for *Machine Quilting Unlimited*, *Quilting Arts*, and *Quilting Arts Gifts* magazines, and she did an instructional DVD through *Quilting Arts*.

"WE CAN WORK IT OUT"

Nancy Firestone • Alexandria, Virginia

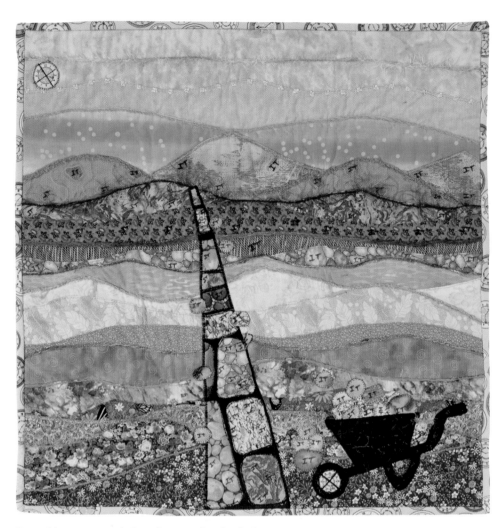

Cotton fabric, yarns; couched, machine-pieced, and quilted.

Nancy is a Beatles fan. When she was twelve, they first arrived on our shores and she grew into adolescence and adulthood with their music. She used to play the piano and presently sings in her church choir. She loves all kinds of music, from pop hits and classical music to hip hop and spiritual. The words of the songs stream through her life and allow her to express her thoughts and emotions on a different level. She is probably the only person who has already selected the songs she wants sung for her funeral, she says; she keeps the list with her will.

Nancy's mother taught her to sew as a child. She made a lot of clothing for herself and, eventually, for her children. Her mother-in-law introduced her to quilting and, in 1976, she made her first quilt. It was hand-appliquéd and hand-quilted. Handwork is not her forte, however; it was years later when she took up quilting again and focused on machine-piecing, appliqué, and quilting. She only began making art quilts in the last five years after taking several classes with wonderful local instructors. She entered her first art quilt into Sacred Threads, a juried show, and adds it was an honor to have her quilt accepted. Some of her quilting friends suggested she sign up for the Beatles challenge, and she was excited to give it a try.

Nancy chose "We Can Work It Out" because of her work as a mental health therapist. Her theory and practice as a therapist is summarized by the lines in this song, she explains. She originally thought her design would involve people in therapy, but the quilt would not cooperate — "it wanted to be a landscape scene with the boulders and rocks as the 'it' that needs to be worked out," she sighs. The path represents the shortness of life. The clocks with the "x" through them, as the sun and wheelbarrow wheel, symbolize the shortness of time. She reveals that drawing outside the lines to make a quilt without a pattern is still daunting for her.

Nancy finds quilting "challenging and relaxing" at the same time. She enjoys the beauty of the fabrics and the subsequent result of combining fabrics into whole new designs. She has a plethora of unfinished quilting projects to get back to, now that this quilt challenge is behind her, and she also plans to complete several charity quilts for her guild. Besides sewing, "I enjoy singing, reading, and spending time with my children and grandchildren."

"WHEN I'M SIXTY-FOUR"

Judy Walsh • Fairfax, Virginia

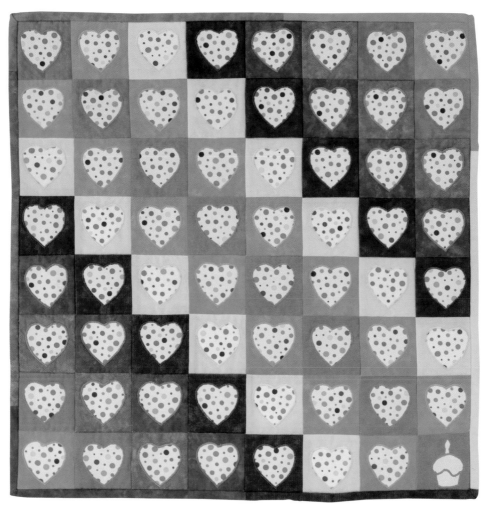

Cotton fabric; machine raw edge appliquéd and quilted.

Judy believes some of the most beautiful music is symphonic recordings of the Beatles: compositions, with no words. She took piano lessons for about eight years as a child, and she and one of her older brothers used to play duets. Whenever anyone asked her to play the piano, she played "Dixie," which was interesting since she grew up in Wisconsin. Today, she enjoys listening to many types of music: country, show tunes, easy listening, and Frank Sinatra. During the day, there is usually music playing somewhere in the house, mostly just for background enjoyment, as she doesn't feel it affects her creative process.

Judy began sewing as a child. Growing up, her mother made all of her clothes. When she was in high school, her mom encouraged her to take a beginning sewing class. Her mom knew Judy would learn better by having a teacher correct her mistakes. Judy loved clothes and knew it would be cheaper to learn to make them than to buy them off of the rack. Over the years, her skills improved and she made most of her own clothes. She did this more for the uniqueness of the clothing

and the joy of accomplishment it brought her, rather than for the economics of making something from scratch.

Judy chose "When I'm Sixty-Four" because she likes the song. She adds that she hears it as a love song. To her, the song means bright colors and light-hearted designs. She thought it would be easy to come up with a concept of a happy quilt. The quilt is made up of sixty-four rainbow-colored squares, sixty-three of which have a bright-colored, polka-dotted heart appliquéd to it. The last square has the birthday greeting, representing achieving the age of sixty-four. Judy, herself, has achieved and enjoyed seventy-four years of life, accompanied by benefits: a cottage on the Isle of Wight, grandchildren, some bottles of wine, and she and her husband still need one another.

Author's Note: Judy was very excited about this project and couldn't wait to see its culmination in this book. Sadly, Judy suddenly passed away in January 2014. We love her and we miss her.

"WHILE MY GUITAR GENTLY WEEPS"

Anne Argentieri • Fairfax Station, Virginia

Cotton fabric, gimp, snaps, fusible web, glass beads, silk thread; fusible machine appliquéd and quilted, hand-appliquéd.

The only time Anne ever listened to mainstream music was while she was doing her homework, listening to the local AM radio station. She vividly recalls one night in March 1963, when she heard a song called "I Want to Hold Your Hand" by some group she had never heard of. She thought how entirely different this band sounded compared to the current rock and roll bands of the time. She loved that new music! Little did she know how big this group would become and that this was the beginning of the British Invasion. When the Beatles came to play at Shea Stadium in 1965, Anne had an opportunity to get a ticket and go with her girlfriends, but she said no thanks. "What was I thinking?" she asks now.

Anne was a "folkie" in high school and college. She owns every Chad Mitchell Trio album ever made, as well as many more by other folk groups. She remains a stout-hearted folk song fan and never owned a Beatles album until she was well into her forties. She chose the song "While My Guitar Gently Weeps" because of her son Michael. He plays the acoustic guitar and she loved listening to him play when he lived at home. She misses him and his guitar-playing. This is her first art quilt "and probably my last," she admits, adding that she could have made two or three baby quilts in the amount of time she spent planning and executing this wall-hanging.

"WHY DON'T WE DO IT IN THE ROAD?"

Karen Mudry Avil • Great Falls, Virginia

Cotton fabric, various threads, fusible web; machine-pieced and quilted.

Yes, Karen is a Beatles fan who likes to listen to everything except for rap music. She played the viola and violin and still plays the piano. Music has a calming effect on her life and, when she is being creative, listening to music helps to generate ideas. She began to sew at age twelve when she took a summer course at Singer. She made her own clothes, eventually including her wedding gown, and then she did alterations and made items for her home. She quilts because it is a fun and rewarding hobby, she says. Inspired by a class she took with Lisa Ellis this past year, she started making art quilts.

When trying to select a song for this challenge, Karen remembered only a few of the songs remaining on the list. Although she could recall the name and tune of this song, this should not imply anything about her! The two lines of this song are what inspired her to make the quilt. She participated in this challenge, she states, "because I am old enough to remember when the Beatles started singing and thought it would be a fun project."

A biomedical engineer, Karen says that if she didn't sew "I would decorate and read." She also enjoys gardening. She mainly makes charity quilts for causes like Operation Kid Comfort and the Alzheimer's Art Quilt Initiative.

Kay Lettau • Annandale, Virginia

Cotton fabrics, embroidery floss; paper foundation pieced, hand-appliquéd, machine-pieced, quilted, and tied.

Kay admits she is more of a Beatles fan now than she was when they first appeared on the music scene. She enjoys show tunes and some country music, and finds classical music "relaxing, if that's what I need." Music also makes time at the gym go much better, she insists.

Kay has been sewing since 1974 when she took a class in Albany, New York. She loves quilting, but doesn't consider herself an art quilter. She participated in this challenge since many of her friends were involved. She chose the song "Wild Honey Pie" because "I wanted something with a curve and points — and a pie seemed like it would work," she explains.

Kay once did sociologic research at the University of Wisconsin. Besides sewing, she also enjoys knitting. She has had some of her traditional quilts published in books and magazines, and she teaches quiltmaking.

"WITH A LITTLE HELP FROM MY FRIENDS"

Judy Gula • Annandale, Virginia

Vintage fabric and findings, mixed media; machine-stitched, couched, hand-embellished.

Judy is a Beatles fan who enjoys music and listens to rock and roll. The song she chose for this challenge is about friends. "I have great friends who help and support me," Judy insists. The vintage photo on her quilt is of an all-female band who are sure to be girlfriends. She likes how the photo has music and friends in a vintage setting; she collages vintage fabrics and various other items when she makes art quilts. She works intuitively, and whispers that her quilt "was created and completed in a day." She is the owner and CEO of Artistic Artifacts and Batik Timbal.

Inge was very much influenced by the Beatles in her teen years. She saw them in concert at the Baltimore Civic Center in 1964 and listened to their music everyday. They really inspired her, she says.

Music has always been an important part of Inge's life. Her mother played the piano for her family regularly, which is one of her fondest memories. Inge played the guitar at parties and small events, which helped her to overcome her shyness and gain popularity in high school. Music has also comforted her in many ways, Inge states, and it helps her to think, can change her mood in an instant, and bring back memories, as well as move her to tears or make her laugh. It always touches her heart, reaches into her soul, inspires creativity, and moves her feet.

Inge started sewing at the age of seven when she learned to make doll clothes. Her grandmother was a seamstress in Germany who inspired Inge and her mother to follow in her footsteps. Imagination and creativity came from Inge's mother, who liked to make toys and crafts from leftover fabric. Inge made her first quilt in 1970, when her daughter was a baby, and began quilting in earnest in 1998, when she joined Quilters Unlimited after attending their annual quilt show. Today, quilting gives her great pleasure. "I love the many patterns, colors, and textures in fabric," she declares, "and it

Cotton fabric, fusible web, lace, various embellishments, acrylic paint; sketched, stamped, hand- and machine-quilted.

challenges me to use my brain and imagination." She also loves to be with other quilters.

Inge maintains she has loved all forms of art since childhood. She attended the Corcoran School of Art as a teen. Today, she works with different types of media and materials and challenges herself to explore everything available. She feels there are no rules when it comes to art, only imagination. She has also been a photographer since her early twenties and enjoys the new world of digital photography. She has had many jobs in her life, but enjoyed none more than working at George Mason University and Northern Virginia Community College. Listening to the ideas of young people just starting out in life who have not yet lost their enthusiasm is refreshing, she explains.

After a lengthy relationship ended in which words were used to deceive, hurt, and manipulate, Inge decided the sweetness of "Words

of Love" would serve as a reminder that not all love is unkind. She hoped focusing on the positive sides of love in this creative process would help to heal her wounds. The inspiration came from within her heart and the desire to be loved. While making this piece, she remembered friends, school, and simpler times when life was fresh and all things were possible. She challenged herself to return to the creative world that she always loved and to free herself from the betrayal she experienced.

In order to complete this quilt, she gave up precious time with her grandchildren. Next on her to-do list? She plans to create special quilts and art quilts for all of the people who stood by her during her difficult transition. She thinks while we are on our journey through life, if we have an opportunity to make a difference in someone else's life, there is no greater gift we can give.

"YELLOW SUBMARINE"

Cheryl P. Stanczyk • Centreville, Virginia

Cheryl is a Beatles fan who listened to their music while growing up in a military family. No matter where her family lived, Beatles' music played. She remembers the songs gaining popularity in the U.S. and to those stationed abroad via military radio stations. These were fond memories and great songs to listen to during times of sorrow when so many military members were actively involved in some way with the Vietnam War.

Cheryl played a musical instrument starting in elementary school and continuing through college. Her love of all things musical helped guide her children into music throughout their school years, and they continue to play instruments today. Music soothes the soul and helps the body relieve the stresses of the day, she says.

Cheryl has been sewing since the age of nine. Both of her grandmothers were amazing seamstresses, and one was also an avid quilter. She still has her grandmother's sewing machine from the 1920s. Cheryl quickly chose "Yellow Submarine" because it was the first song that popped into her mind. The song conjures memories of growing up in the military, being nine years old, and living in Okinawa. Her older sister listened to the radio a lot and Cheryl remembered this song, in particular, playing numerous times a day. The words of the song inspired this quilt, which

Cotton fabric, Angelina, crystals, sequins, spangles, buttons, various fibers and other embellishments; machine-pieced and quilted, hand-embellished.

was the start of art quilting for her. "I had fun reading the lyrics of the song and interpreting the meaning of them," Cheryl reveals. Panic soon set in, though, and she worried she wouldn't be able to create a quality product, as she discovered art quilting takes a lot more work than making a traditional quilt. Since there is no repetition of design, it requires more thinking things out before sewing.

Quilting is only one of Cheryl's hobbies. As a military spouse, she has found things to do to occupy her time, especially since she has constantly moved from one location to another. She seeks out friendships with people who share common interests, and she has been able to find those special friendships through quilting and being a part of quilt guilds around the country.

Cheryl worked as a transit planner in Grand Forks, North Dakota, and Biloxi, Mississippi. She wrote proposals and documents to get funding for transit Park and Rides. Besides quilting, she shows her two Kerry Blue Terriers in AKC dog shows, achieving championships and certifications in herding and rally. Her older dog is also a therapy dog and spends time with children at the local library once a month.

If she didn't sew, Cheryl says, "I would be really bored." She confesses she can't sit idle; she always needs to do some sort of handwork. Her next project: Start making blocks for a retirement quilt for her husband, who will soon have thirty years in the air force. Cheryl is the mother of two sons; the older one recently married. The younger one will marry in 2014; he plans to enter the air force's medical services corps, following in the footsteps of his father and grandfather, doing service for our country.

Martha Fitzpatrick • Springfield, Virginia

Cotton fabrics, fusible web; machine-appliquéd, quilted.

Although she is not really a Beatles fan, Martha contends, she does like some of their songs. She took piano lessons as a child and was in chorus in high school and college. She enjoys listening to classical music because she finds it soothing.

Martha learned to sew as a child in the 4-H club. She mostly sewed clothes until the early 1980s, when she started quilting. She chose "Yesterday" because it was the first song that came to mind and it was still available. The inspiration for it came when she remembered back to the '60s and thought of hippies. She usually makes traditional quilts, so this one is atypical because it is her first art quilt, she states.

Martha taught English, worked in a library, sold Avon, and was an office temp in the past. Besides quilting, she reads and volunteers at the library. If she didn't sew, she says, "I would probably do tole painting."

"YOU REALLY GOT A HOLD ON ME"

Annabel Ebersole • Williamsburg, Virginia

Cotton fabric, wool, screws, silk fibers, beads, elastic; hand-appliquéd, beaded, machine-appliquéd, and quilted.

Music by the Beatles was such an integral part of her growing up, Annabel says. She had a crush on George. Annabel lived in London for four years and says it was exciting to live close to Abbey Road and see the studios.

Annabel and her husband are groupies of some modern classical music groups, and they still enjoy going to see his college band, The Studs, perform. Although she doesn't play any musical instruments herself, she maintains, "I can clap a lot for men in their sixties playing music of the '60s."

Annabel, who began quilting twenty-eight years ago in Brazil, was intrigued by art quilts. She took classes with artist Judy House and has attended the Quilt Surface Design Symposium in Columbus, Ohio, many times. Ultimately, she began to teach art quilting. Working in two quilt shops gave her knowledge of and exposure to many art quilters in the area. The ability to quilt flows through her and out her

fingertips, Annabel believes, and she views this as a divine gift. Many of her quilts are hanging in cancer or diabetes treatment centers. "As an artist, this is how I can lift up those living with diseases," she states.

The song "You Really Got A Hold On Me" speaks of being together with her wonderful husband, Bruce, with the kids in her new neighborhood, and with Bruce's college friends, who play guitars just like the one in her quilt. She included pieces of fabric and fibers in this quilt from different experiences in her life. Most of her quilts are similar to this one: colorful with three-dimensional embellishments.

Annabel and her husband are in a time of transition since their move from northern Virginia to Williamsburg. While making this quilt, she had the exhilarating experience of being on the committee for the Sacred Threads Exhibit, she divulges. She is also a member of Fiber Artists @ Loose Ends, ArtQuiltNetwork, Quilt Alliance, SAQA, and local guilds.

"YOU'VE GOT TO HIDE YOUR LOVE AWAY"

Lisa Purdy • Woodbridge, Virginia

Cotton, satin, upholstery fabric, yarn, sequins, dyed horsetail hair; machine-appliquéd and quilted.

Lisa is a Beatles fan whose daughter's name is Michelle. She often serenaded her to sleep by singing her the Beatles song, "Michelle." She listens to all kinds of music because it provokes happiness, dancing, and good memories.

Lisa started sewing clothes as a teenager, taught by her mother. Years later, she admired her friend Kris' art quilts; Kris and another friend, Nancy, became her quilting instructors. She listened to many, many Beatles songs before settling on "You've Got to Hide Your Love

Away" for the this quilt challenge. She was inspired more by the lyrics of the song rather than the title. Her quilt depicts a heartbroken young man who has been rejected in love. The lyrics describe his loss, and they also mention the clowns she portrayed on the quilt. Lisa paints in oils and says quilting is another medium that allows her to express her artistic being. She finds working in fiber is an enjoyable challenge. Lisa would like to thank Kris Bishop for sharing her fabric and Nancy Jones for sharing her sewing machine and for her unfailing cheerfulness.

APPLIQUÉ: To sew a fabric cut in a particular shape onto a background by hand or sewing machine.

ART QUILT: To use sewing techniques and materials to create something imaginative.

BATIK: A special kind of fabric woven tighter than regular cotton fabric; designed with an Indonesian method of printing, sometimes featuring rich and saturated colors.

BATTING: The inside of a quilt.

BINDING: The outermost narrow finished edge of a quilt.

COUCHED: A method of attaching fibers, to include yarns, ribbons, and/or threads to a larger background; it's done either by hand or using a sewing machine. This is usually a decorative element.

CRAZY QUILTING: A random kind of patchwork sometimes using nontraditional fabrics and decorative stitching as embellishment.

EMBELLISH: To add stitching, doodads, or bling to a piece; to use any of a number of materials and/or techniques to garnish.

EMBROIDERY: Fancy stitching done by hand or sewing machine using special decorative thread, to add interest.

FREE MOTION: A technique in sewing where a person disables the mechanism on a sewing machine, which normally causes the machine to operate in a straight line, so the operator can guide the fabric freely with the hands, in effect using the sewing machine to draw on a piece of fabric.

FUSED: To iron a commercial specialty web onto the back of a piece of fabric and iron it onto another piece of fabric so both pieces adhere.

HAND-DYED FABRIC: Cloth that is specially colored using one of various dyeing techniques.

HAND-PIECING: To sew pieces of fabric together by hand.

JURY: A committee formed to judge which quilts to include in an exhibit or project.

LAMÉ: A thin, shiny metallic fabric, usually silver or gold, sometimes known as "floozy fabric."

LONGARM SEWING MACHINE: A ten- to fourteen-foot-long industrial sewing machine, complete with rollers to hold layers of fabric and batting. The operator of this machine uses it to sew the layers of fabric into a quilt. With this type of machine, it is possible to more easily accomplish this task when a quilt is very large or when a particular custom design is desired. One of these machines costs a pretty penny. People who use longarm quilters pay them to complete this part of their quilts.

MACHINE-PIECING: To sew pieces of cloth together with a sewing machine.

MODERN QUILT: Functional quilts often made of solid fabrics and vivid colors; these quilts make use of negative space, asymmetry, and modern design.

PAPER-PIECING: A method of using a pattern to precisely sew pieces of fabric together by stitching cloth to paper and then discarding the paper.

QUILT POLICE: A possibly mythical group of monitors and judges who verify all quilters strictly follow "traditional rules" of quilting. Many of the artists included in this book have lived in fear of these operatives all of their stitching lives. The lucky ones have broken free of the clutches of the Quilt Police.

QUARTER-INCH SEAM: The widely recognized standard seam width in the world of traditional quilts; strictly monitored by the Quilt Police.

QUILTED: Sewn through the three layers of a quilt to hold it all together. May be done by hand or sewing machine; sometimes the pattern is stitched in a decorative design, sometimes this is just done for utility.

QUILTING BEE: People who come together on an informal basis, sharing an interest in quilting.

QUILT GUILD: A membership organization of quilters.

ROTARY CUTTER: A special tool with a very sharp circular blade used instead of scissors to cut fabric. Not to be confused with a pizza cutter.

SAMPLER QUILT: A traditional quilt where each block is a different pattern.

SLEEVE: A fabric casing sewn onto the back of a quilt used for ease of hanging on a wall.

STASH: A collection of fabric of varying amounts, colors, and styles, gathered for eventual use. At times, this is something quilters feel compelled to hide, purge, make excuses for, or disperse around the house to make it look like less than it is.

STUMPWORK: A way to stitch fabric to give it a three-dimensional effect.

TRADITIONAL QUILT: Quilts often based on block patterns that have been used for a hundred years or more.

TREADLE MACHINE: The old-fashioned kind of sewing machine that our grandmothers used, operated by pressing the foot on a small, flat bar.

WHOLE CLOTH: Not pieced; only using one piece of fabric.

ABOUT QUILTING

Quilt Shows

If you are interested in visiting a quilt show, and possibly seeing these Beatles quilts or other quilts in person, here are some popular quilt shows, with approximate dates. Search these shows on the Internet for specific information about dates, locations, and special exhibits. This is not a comprehensive list.

AMERICAN QUILTER'S SOCIETY
Charlotte, NC (late July/early August)
Chattanooga, TN (mid-September)
Des Moines, IA (early October)
Grand Rapids, MI (late August)
Lancaster, PA (mid-March)
Paducah, KY (late April)
Phoenix, AZ (early February)

DENVER NATIONAL QUILT FESTIVAL
Denver, CO (early May)

INTERNATIONAL QUILT FESTIVALS
Chicago, IL (mid-June)
Houston, TX (late October, early November)
Long Beach, CA (early August)

KANSAS CITY REGIONAL QUILT FESTIVAL
Overland Park, KS (mid-June, every other year)

MID-ATLANTIC QUILT FESTIVAL
Hampton, VA (late February to early March)

ORIGINAL SEWING AND QUILT EXPO
Birmingham, AL (mid-October)
Fort Worth, TX (mid-October)
Fredericksburg, VA (early October)
Minneapolis, MN (early November)
Overland Park, KS (late November)

PACIFIC INTERNATIONAL QUILT FESTIVAL
Santa Clara, CA (mid-October)

PENNSYLVANIA NATIONAL QUILT EXTRAVAGANZA
Philadelphia, PA (late September)

QUILT FEST OF NEW JERSEY
Somerset, NJ (early March)

QUILT FEST OASIS
Palm Springs, CA (early October)

QUILT FEST DESTINATION SAVANNAH
Savannah, GA (late March)

QUILT! KNIT! STITCH!
Portland, OR (mid-August)

QUILT NATIONAL
Athens, OH (late May through early September)

QUILT ODYSSEY
Hershey, PA (late July)

QUILTERS UNLIMITED QUILT SHOW
Chantilly, VA (late May to early June)

ROAD TO CALIFORNIA
Ontario, CA (late January)

ROCKY MOUNTAIN QUILT FESTIVAL
Loveland, CO (mid-August)

SACRED THREADS EXHIBIT
Herndon, VA (mid-July, every other year)

SISTERS OUTDOOR QUILT SHOW
Sisters, OR (mid-July)

VERMONT QUILT FESTIVAL
Essex Junction, VT (late June)

WISCONSIN QUILT EXPO
Madison, WI (mid-September)

WORLD QUILT SHOW
West Palm Beach, FL (early January)

WORLD QUILT SHOW NEW ENGLAND
Manchester, NH (mid-August)

Learn More About Quilting

If you are not a quilter, but would like to learn more about quilting, there are several possibilities. You can seek out quilt shows and exhibits, including those held in museums, and there are national memberships you could explore. Look on the Internet for current and specific information on what these organizations offer:

- **AMERICAN QUILTER'S SOCIETY**
- **MODERN QUILT GUILD**
- **NATIONAL QUILTING ASSOCIATION**
- **QUILT ALLIANCE**
- **STUDIO ART QUILT ASSOCIATES, INC.**

You might want to find out if there is a local guild of quilters in your area. Go to fabric, quilting, or craft stores and check their bulletin boards. Ask customers and cashiers if they know of any groups or find out if the store is offering any classes.

Books and online tutorials abound, so you can also teach yourself some things. Check out Academy of Quilting (formerly Quilt University) and Craftsy®, both online options. Many times, when I have wanted to learn more about something specific, or when I get stuck, I do a search on YouTube® and discover the solution right there.

Public Broadcasting Stations and cable television are other places to find programs on quilting.

If you would like to belong to a group, but can't find one to join, start your own — it's that simple. Figure out a place to meet where everyone will be comfortable, look for people, and establish some guidelines of how you want your meetings to be formatted.

Above all else, don't feel you need to be a master quilter to join a group. Most welcome anyone with an interest.

Donate Your Quilts to Charities

Many of the participants in this book work very diligently to make quilts to donate to worthy causes. If you are a quilter and would like to donate, here are some ideas for organizations in need. Obtain up-to-date contact information on the Internet.

- **ALZHEIMER'S QUILT INITIATIVE**
- **AMERICAN RED CROSS**
- **ARMED SERVICES**
- **CATHOLIC CHARITIES**
- **OPERATION KID COMFORT**
- **PROJECT LINUS**
- **QUILTS OF VALOR**

In addition to the above, it is never hard to find people in need. Homeless shelters, battered women shelters, halfway houses, group homes, and hospital NICU and cancer centers often welcome donations of quilts. Keep your eyes open for communities that suffer from natural or man-made disaster; listen for contact information so you know the collection point for these quilts. You might also want to inquire at animal hospitals.

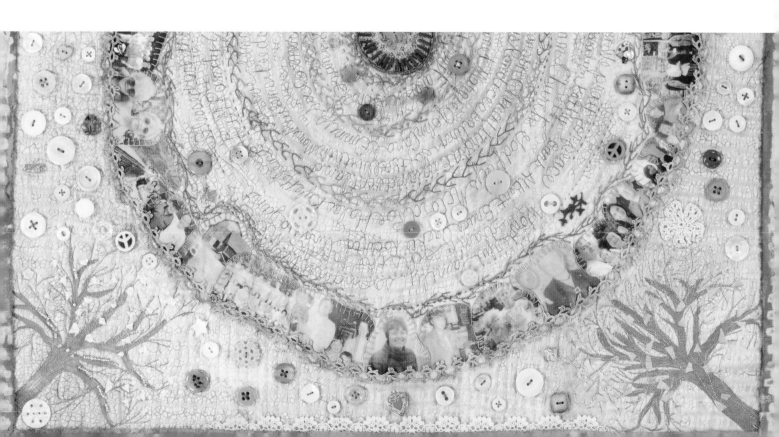

ARTIST INDEX

For information on how to reach any of these artists, email author at fiberbeatles@gmail.com.

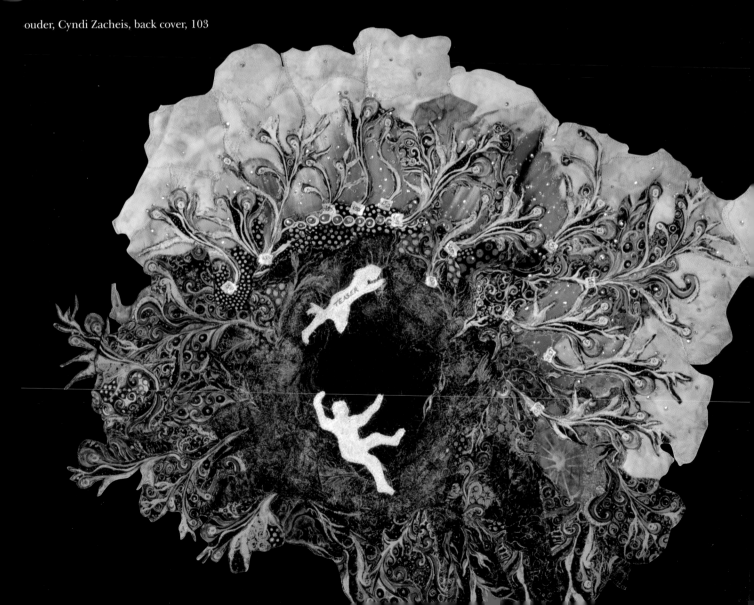

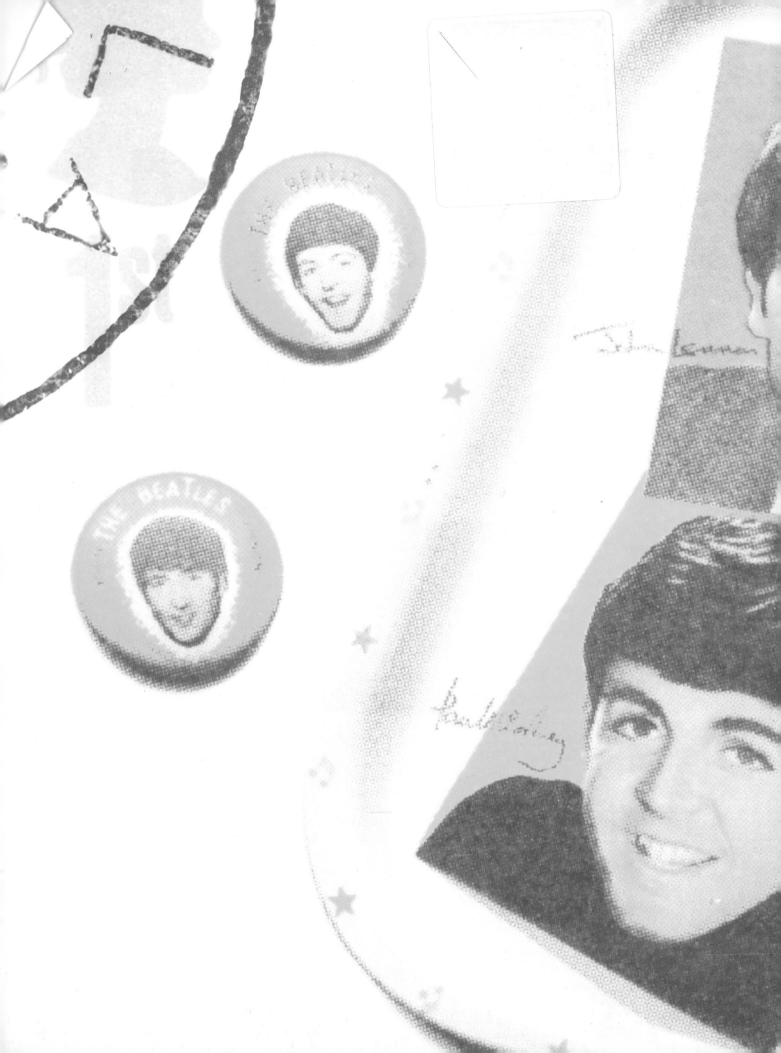